Memories
of
Harrogate

Part of the
Memories
series

Memories

of

Harrogate

Edited by Margaret Power

The Publishers would like to thank the following companies
for supporting the production of this book

Allens of Harrogate

Bettys & Taylors of Harrogate

Albert Hymas Limited

Ogden of Harrogate

Smiths the Rink Limited

First published in Great Britain by True North Books Limited
Units 3 - 5 Heathfield Industrial Park
Elland West Yorkshire
HX5 9AE
Tel. 01422 377977
© Copyright: True North Books Limited 2000

ISBN 1 903204 01 1

Text, design and origination by True North Books Limited
Printed and bound by The Amadeus Press Limited

Memories are made of this

Memories. We all have them: people, places and events, some good and some bad. Our memories of the place where we grew up are usually tucked away in a very special place in our mind. The best are probably connected with our childhood and youth, when we longed to be grown up and paid no attention to adults who told us to enjoy being young, as these were the best years of our lives. We look back now and realise that they were right.

Old photographs bring our memories flooding back - coronations and celebrations; talking pictures, Technicolor and television; the war years, rationing, and the shared hopes and fears which created such a warm community spirit; buying things made of nylon and plastic; fashions which took trouserbottoms and hemlines from drainpipes and mini-skirts to the other

extreme; Doris Day, Acker Bilk, Elvis Presley and the Beatles; the jitterbug, the tango and discos; Ford Populars and Minis; decimalisation. Life changed so much over the years. Some changes were big, some small; some altered our lives in ways we never anticipated. Who in the early days of motoring could have foreseen the motorways and traffic systems of the latter decades of the 20th century? Did any of us realise, when we first saw a computer, what a tremendous impact they would have on our lives?

Self-service supermarkets and frozen food made our lives easier - but at the expense of our friendly little corner shops. Nostalgia is always such a mixture of feelings . . . We hope that the collection of pictures in this book will remind you of happy days in bygone eras - and who knows, you might even have been there when one of the photographs was taken!

Contents

Harrogate through the years

The best memories are just around the corner of your mind. They can play tricks on you trying to remember what it was like in the past. But, the camera never lies. Captured in this book are images of Harrogate as it has developed over the last century. Helped by the captions to each photograph, we can stir those thoughts of yesteryear and picture the town as it has grown through time. Once a group of little hamlets, it was launched on its way to becoming that 'Mecca of spa towns', by the discovery of the spring waters in the late 16th century. Turn the pages and wallow in thoughts of Victorians taking the waters and covering themselves in mud poultices. Recall how Harrogate's ancestors thought so far ahead as to protect the open spaces around the town. But for them, the Stray, that lets people walk on its lawns and smell its fragrant flowers, might be a motorway or housing estate.

The days of the elegant baths and their pump rooms are captured forever in this book. You can almost hear again the piano of Paderewski or the golden voice of Dame Nellie Melba in the Royal Hall. Share once more in the peacefulness that is the Valley Gardens and enjoy the special treat that is to be found at the famous Betty's Tea Room. Harrogate is now a thriving conference and exhibition centre. The thousands who pour in to join in the debates and to show off their wares can share with the rest of us in seeing the foundations on which the fame and success of Harrogate were built.

From the excitement of street parties to the sober reflections on the war memorial, happiness and sadness are linked in all our thoughts. These sentiments will come back as you leaf your way through this celebration of one of Yorkshire's most heralded towns. Unusual events lie side by side with the commonplace. Even younger readers will have heard of the famed crime writer, Dame Agatha Christie. The story of her disappearance and discovery in Harrogate in 1926 was filmed here in a movie starring Vanessa Redgrave. That incident and many more will be found in the following pages. Dip in and let the nostalgia roll all over you. But, as you do, remember that history is continuing to be made with every passing moment. That snapshot you take today or that letter you write tomorrow might just be part of a trip down memory lane for someone else in a hundred years' time. Point the lens carefully and put down the words accurately. We all have a part to play in providing a heritage for our children. This book is just one small part of that. However, without the pictures and the words that highlight them, so much would be lost. Remind the young of how it used to be and enjoy what has been preserved in this book for you.

Around the town centre

The Royal Baths on the corner of Crescent Road opened on 3rd July 1897

Looking down on Parliament Street from the junction with Kings Road and Crescent Road, signs of affluence can be seen in the number of cars on the streets. They were the privilege of the well off in the early days of the last century. They mixed happily with the traditional horse drawn vehicles. Elegant women, in sweeping full length Edwardian dresses and delightfully feminine hats, promenaded along the wide pavements outside the variety of shops. The street leads uphill towards the Café Imperial that opened around 1900 and became the site of many a genteel meeting place. On the corner of Kings Road ladies could shop for more fine things to wear. Madge Farlow specialised in blouses, underclothing and children's millinery. Fine high necked blouses were fashionable for women of this period who seldom exposed their skin when out and about in polite society. The dainty parasol was both useful as protection from the sun and as a fashionable item. The banner across Parliament Street advertises the current attraction at the Kursaal. RA Roberts, billed as the greatest protean actor, was making his farewell visit. He was appearing nightly and twice on Saturdays. In Greek myth Proteus was the old man who could take on any form and Mr Roberts would play the parts of all the characters in the play, with the changes effected so quickly they were hardly noticeable to his audience. The Royal Baths, on the corner of Crescent Road, opened on 3 July 1897. This was a month after Queen Victoria's diamond jubilee.

CARS, CHAOS AND COST

Britain saw its first car in 1894. Twenty years later, in 1914, the world's first traffic lights were installed in front of the House of Commons. Cars were here to stay - but they brought with them their own particular problems.

As traffic levels increased in town centres around the country, various schemes were put in place to control the flow. Some involved the motorist's pocket; in 1947 a Road Tax of £1 per year was imposed.

Road safety also became a major issue, and in 1956 the Ministry of Transport introduced road testing, which at first only affected cars more than ten years old.

To the frustration of the many motorists who were used to free parking, parking meters were introduced to Britain in June, 1958. At the same time, yellow no-waiting lines came into force. A whole new way of life began for the British driver.

ooking south along Ripon Road and into Parliament Street, traffic 70 years ago was starting to build up on this busy entry route to the town centre. As the main road towards Leeds and Bradford, this thoroughfare has always been a problem for the road user. Even in those far off days it was necessary to have a bobby keeping things moving at the junction with Kings Road. One way systems and road widening later in the 20th century helped to undo the bottlenecks, but it is still choc a bloc at peak times. That is the price of popularity as Harrogate attracts visitors from all

over the world. On the left, the Royal Hall dominates the scene. It opened in 1903 and is still a major attraction in the town. As a theatre with 1,276 seats it plays host to many musical and cultural events, being considered to be part of the International Centre that appeared in 1981. When the hall first opened, its boards were graced by such greats as Sarah Bernhardt. The 'divine Sarah', as she loved to be called, was 59 when she appeared in 'La dame aux camelias'. The French actress had reigned supreme across the European stage for many years. For her to visit the Royal Hall, or the Kursaal as it then was, established the theatre on a national footing. Julian Clifford was the conductor of the municipal orchestra and he engineered the coming of famous names from the music world to perform here, as well.

*T*his is Harrogate at its best. Prospect Gardens are awash with colour from the well laid out flowerbeds. You can almost smell the perfume of the delicate blooms that beautifully set off the quiet and calm of the hedged garden in front. Here, people could sit and just enjoy the peacefulness of the surroundings. The shiny motor cars of the 1920s bowl along Parliament Street; a busy place even then. The picture was taken from the Alexandra Hotel. Even that name suggests a grandeur that was Harrogate in between the two world wars. The building is now part of a national pub chain and called the Rat and Parrot. Very modern, very trendy - but what would

Queen Alexandra have made of the name? The magnificent architecture beyond the gardens, at the top of Montpellier Parade, stands proudly as if to say, 'I am what this town is about'. The little clock on the turret tells you it is time for tea. Where better to take it than at Betty's Café below? The late Victorian building, once the Café Imperial, is known the length and breadth of the country. Guiseley can have its Harry Ramsden's and fish and chips. Sophisticated Harrogate has Betty's. Its cream cakes and delicious teas keep residents and visitors in touch with a time that is lost but an atmosphere that must be kept. No amount of rats and parrots can take it away.

Below: Thomas Smith, the removal man, had his premises on the corner of Bower Road. As well as offering a house contents removal service, things could also be put into store until they were needed. This was no fly by night company operating a one van service. Smith's was a bigger concern and had a number of vehicles whizzing around the town's streets. Before the days of motorised transport, possessions went by horse drawn cart. People did not own so much in the way of furniture and equipment as those in the 21st century. There was little movement away from the place of birth as families were often born, lived and died in the same house. The petrol engine provided the chance to go further afield for work and leisure. New homes were set up well away from the birthplace and the removal of personal goods and chattels became a growth area. Before long the Smith vans were speeding their way across the country and even developed an overseas service. Business reputation counted for a great deal. In what was one of the most stressful experiences a person could have, a house move had to be as efficient as possible. Horror stories of 'Right said Fred' style of furniture removal made house-holders anxious that their valuable and fragile knickknacks would not survive the move. 'Do you know that piano is on my foot?' 'No, but if you hum it I'll be able to join in' was not appreciated.

Station Square, as it looked in the middle of the 20th century, was to undergo some major changes in the 1950s. When this photograph was taken the place still had quite an open feel to it. That was not to last. This row of shops would disappear to make way for the development of the Victoria Gardens Centre. Later, the Coptall Tower development would arrive and loom over the square

like some ugly giant. Howden's, the business on the right, called itself 'the most complete northern motor service'. Its reputation did not save it from the march of so-called progress and it was demolished along with the rest. Station Square, though tucked away in the middle of town, is still an important spot in the town. As it boasts access to and from the bus and railway stations, it has a large volume of people

GLASS, STEEL AND CONCRETE

Clearance schemes were in place even before World War II, and overcrowded homes with no bathrooms and outside toilets were demolished. In 1939 around 350,000 new homes were built.

The end of World War II saw the creation of a green belt around London where building would be prohibited. Fourteen new towns were developed during the 1940s - followed by fourteen more in the 1960s - to deal with London's 'overspill'.

Between 1955 and 1975 town and city centres around the country were transformed as rows of Victorian shops, pubs and homes were swept away to make way for modern buildings.

It was the Festival of Britain in 1951 which brought about drastic changes in architectural design. The 300ft-high Skylon, shaped like an enormous cigar, soared above the exhibition grounds and was visible for miles around.

crossing its way each day. As the home of the impressive Victoria monument, the square attracts visitors seeking out the various aspects of Harrogate's history. Mayor Richard Ellis put it up in 1887 to mark the queen's golden jubilee. When this picture was taken, petrol rationing was still in force. Private car ownership was the privilege of only a few. The quiet scene contrasts with the bumper to bumper traffic you will experience there today. Some people call that progress. It seems an odd description. How can you progress whilst at a standstill?

Bottom: Albert Street runs from Prospect Place up to Station Parade. It looks very different today from this 1938 scene. The cars and vans of the era look like Dinky toys compared with the large petrol guzzling machines of the 21st century. A lifetime ago these little boxes on wheels were the state of the art. You could have any colour you wanted, as long as it was black. It is a damp and gloomy March day and there is little to liven the mood. Even the news from abroad is not too good. Hitler's troops have gone into Austria. At home there is unrest. Anthony Eden has resigned as Foreign Secretary. He thought that the prime minister, Neville Chamberlain, was too soft in his talks with the Fuhrer and Mussolini. How right he was in the long run. At least we can enjoy listening to some good music of the time. HMV radios, being advertised on the billboard at Falshaws, could transmit the company's latest record releases for us. Who can ever think of HMV without recalling its famous logo? The little dog, Nipper, listening to the sounds coming from the horn on the gramophone was a wonderful idea. When the company was launched in 1931, the idea of linking His Master's Voice with Nipper was a master stroke. Classic tunes like 'September in the rain' and 'The folks who live on the hill' were brought to us by the wireless that was the main source of family entertainment. Further along is the Co-op, absorbed by Harrogate and District CWS, where we could get some 'divi' on our purchases.

Right: The debris in front of the market hall provides an ugly foreground to the picture. The cars and vans beyond show the austerity of the times. It is 1950 and the war years have not been gone for long. Britain is rebuilding and this is no time for flash motors. They will come later, with their bright colours and gleaming chrome. In the meantime, practicality is what is required. Rationing is in force and petrol, food and clothing in short supply. Resources need to be stretched and bargains in the market are essential to keep the family fed and dressed adequately. Car owners needed vehicles that were economical in fuel consumption. The market was the second such building on this site and here we are looking at the entrance from Station Parade. It had been erected in 1939. Built of artificial stone as an economy measure, it was being enlarged when this scene was captured. A row of shops was demolished to make way for the new development that had a definite postwar style about it. At the same time Station Square was made more spacious. The remodelled market hall lasted until 1991. In February of that year it joined the rubble in front of it in this photograph. It was demolished and replaced by the Victoria Gardens shopping development. This development cost over £50 million and covers some 90,000 square feet. It opened in 1992.

The leafy boulevards of the crossroads where the Leeds-Ripon and Otley-Knaresborough meet make an attractive summertime scene. Elsewhere in Europe the storm clouds are gathering. It is May 1939. Soon, the sunny days will be gone and the lightning strikes of the blitzkrieg will turn the world upside down, once again. Before those days come, there is work to do on the old turnpike roads. Increasing traffic flow into town caused the council great headaches. It was not too good for the locals or visiting motorists either. The junction, known as Prince of Wales corner, is in the process of being widened. Marking out is taking place on the Leeds Road side. Shortly, the traffic lights will be taken away and a pleasing flowerbed and roundabout installed. The edges of the Stray were to be taken over in order to extend the approach. The Prince of Wales Hotel, from where the photograph was taken, was built by Michael Hattersley in 1815. He named it after himself and it was soon established as an important posting house. Later the Brunswick, it gained its royal name in 1866. In the 1830s a Mrs Waudby owned it. She married a certain Henry Peacock. He had been sacked as governor of the workhouse, but rallied to become   one of the improvement commissioners. Financial problems, never fully explained, caused him to make a rapid exit from public and publican life in 1849. The building is now called the Prince of Wales Mansions and houses a set of flats.

At leisure

Roll out those lazy, hazy, crazy days of summer. Note how the hemlines have started to creep up since before the first world war. They were now at mid calf level. The country was enjoying the final balmy summer days on 18 September 1926 and nowhere more happily than in the Valley Gardens. People relaxed on park benches, strolled in the sunshine and children would splash about in the paddling pool. This was a place where the problems of the outside world could be forgotten. The general strike in May had come as a shock when a state of emergency was declared. The use of troops to keep order in parts of Scotland and south Wales did not seem to be part of the British way of life. Fortunately, it was mainly limited to the industrial areas. Even so, Harrogate residents saw some of the effects in fuel and food shortages. But, those were not to be thought of on a day like this. There was a band playing and the crowds could sit back and enjoy the music. A rousing Sousa march, like 'Liberty Bell' or 'Washington Post' would get feet tapping. The strains of 'Three little maids from school' from Gilbert and Sullivan's 'Mikado' had us humming along. Sometimes, a band would show off its knowledge of modern pop music and blast out 'Bye-bye blackbird'. Wafting across the pines there came the strains of a tune by some new chap called Gershwin. Wonder if his music will catch on?

Below: Autumn browns and golds were starting to form on 8 September 1926. Looking over the top of the 1858 Gothic pump room that is the Magnesia Well, there is a lovely view of the Valley Gardens. The beautifully kept flowerbeds and manicured lawns are seen at their best. The pathways were laid out in such a way that they could be viewed in pretty patterns radiating from the central section. Visitors to the gardens often continue their walk by going on through the Pine Woods. Passing through this fragrant area is a pleasure in itself. The enjoyment is heightened when reaching the marvellous Harlow Carr botanical gardens, home to the Northern Horticultural Society. The Valley Gardens were especially popular with Victorian society. Women in long, swishing dresses, shading their heads with dainty parasols, strolled here with top hatted gentry. They would be holding silver topped canes and the whole scene was one of exquisite elegance. So popular did the gardens become that they were enlarged in 1901. In later years many visitors from overseas would enjoy the delights of the gardens. During the last war American visitors loved to enjoy what the gardens had to offer. The peace and tranquillity of this spot was so different from the skyscrapers back home. All the noise and pain of modern warfare could be forgotten for a while. There is a plaque at the entrance to the gardens that records what was felt. 'This tablet was erected by officers and nurses of the 216th General Hospital of the US Army ... who spent happy days in Harrogate ... July 28 1944 - May 11 1945'.

Right: The first world war could have been a century away when looking at this scene. In fact, it is 1920 and the guns have only been silent for two years. Yet, the idyllic spot that is the Valley Gardens shows no trace of the death and destruction that ripped apart so much of our world. This is how life should always be. Tree lined avenues, the branches full of bird song and a green land that is forever England. It was to preserve this that so many went overseas to earn our freedom. The sad part of it is that over 800 of the town's brave souls never returned to enjoy the freedom they had won. Thanks to them we could visit the Magnesia Pump Room on the right or head towards the Old Sulphur Well under the Royal Pump Room at the entrance to the gardens. Just as importantly, we had the time and opportunity to soak up the beauty of this spot. The freedom to enjoy the acres of glorious gardens, the colourful floral displays and the open spaces was worth fighting for. What other town could rival the natural beauty and dignified architecture that was, and still is, Harrogate? Even the buildings overlooking the gardens add majesty to the scene. They add a certain distinction to the tranquil nature of the gardens, suiting each other so well.

Below: *The remains of the Magnesia Pump Room look forlorn alongside the bright summer flowers and leafy bushes. The Valley Gardens, home to many medicinal springs, was proud of its springs and wells. They helped to bring prosperity to the town. Visitors came in droves to 'spaw', as the practice of taking the waters was known. By the time of the Victorian era, Harrogate had become not just the premier spa town in England, but of the whole British Empire. So universal was its fame that perhaps only the baths in Vittel, in eastern France, could be considered a serious challenger. It was in Low Harrogate that the waters became the most popular. It had been in High Harrogate that the first wells had been discovered. It was as long ago as 1571 that the Tewit Spring was first found to have medicinal properties. John Slingsby discovered it by accident when he stumbled across it. He realised that the taste of the water reminded him of those springs he had sampled on the continent. His discovery is remembered in the domed building on the Stray, just off Leeds Road. But, it was the discovery of the numerous springs around what is now Valley Gardens that brought the influx of visitors and interest in the 17th and 18th centuries. Rising from deep under the ground, the waters brought with them the medicinal minerals that our ancestors swore by to cure gout, rheumatism and a host of other ailments. Pictured on 4 August 1924, the Magnesia Well was one such popular site. Restored after this fire, it was again gutted in 1983. It is now a café.*

Manchester's famous Hallé orchestra, the brainchild of the German born Charles (Carl) Hallé around 1858, was but one of a series of prominent visitors to the Royal Hall. Dame Nellie Melba sang here, the proud son of Shropshire, Edward German, conducted the orchestra and the Polish virtuoso Jan Paderewski tinkled the ivories on the Royal Hall's grand piano. There were also less highbrow shows put on. The advert for 'No no Nanette' publicises a musical written in 1925 by Vincent (Millie) Youmans. He wrote such other classic musicals and songs as 'Flying down to Rio' and 'Tea for two'. Pictured in the 1940s, the Royal Hall had begun life as the Kursaal. The original name can still be seen in relief high above the main entrance. Kursaals were fashionable German buildings in spa towns on the continent. The borrowed name was used until the first world war. Not surprisingly, the German link was then dropped for something more patriotic. The idea for the Kursaal came from Dr Black in 1898. He suggested a concert room for over 2,000 people, a games room and reading room. Rates were 5 shillings (25p) in the pound and the council had a debt of £250,000. Townspeople were horrified at the expense. Even so, council members went off to the continent to study the model Kursaals over there. Junketing is not something new. They returned to recommend a modified plan. RJ Beale and F Matcham designed the building, on the corner of Kings Road and Ripon Road. It opened in 1903.

Left: The once impressive dome and facade of the Magnesia Well were wrecked in a fire in August 1924. Situated just beyond a small pool in the Valley Gardens, the pump room had been erected in 1895. It was immediately popular and was one of the best loved spots for a visit at the turn into the 20th century. The body language of those gazing at the remains shows how shocked the people were. Even the young boy facing the camera strikes a glum pose as he joins in with the feeling of gloom about what has happened. This especially pretty part of the gardens was a favourite haunt of those wanting to experience the curative powers of the spa waters. Perhaps the little throng by the Magnesia Pump Room had been hoping to relax there. Instead, they gather in joint mourning. The dress of the period showed both men and women favouring wide brims on their hats. The age of smaller homburgs and flappers' bonnets was not too far away. Hemlines were starting to creep up. The floor touching dresses of Edwardian times had been replaced by a fashion that allowed a woman to display a neatly turned calf. Thankfully, the turnups on the men's trousers remained firmly at shoe level. The shock of any male legs, other than those of a youngster, being on view would have been too much for polite society to bear.

Above: Skiing at Klosters or belting down the Cresta Run at St Moritz was not on the agenda for this family. But, it could have its own fun at home. Winter sports had come to Harlow Moor Drive. This four man bobsled was getting some good use in the chilly surroundings. Woolly scarves and hats were the order of the day. The driver looks to be tough nut. No gloves for him. What would he have thought of the modern footballer who runs out onto the pitch in gloves and tights when the temperature drops a couple of degrees? They made them tougher in the old days. They made games more fun as well. As soon as the snow settled out came the home made sleighs. Snowball fights were underway and dad's pipe was pinched to put in the snowman's mouth. Tingling feet and fingers with frosted breath hanging in the air were just part and parcel of the occasion. Even if you did not have a sled that had been knocked up in the back shed, an old tin tray would do just as well. Then it was off down the street or to the nearest hillside. How many times have you nearly lost your kneecaps to little scallywag hurtling down the slope, with or without his toboggan? It was all an expected part of the fun. Eventually, it was back home for a mug of steaming Bovril. Keep your greenhouse effect and give us back our ice age.

SOUND AND VISION

The first radio broadcast *was made by the BBC on 15th November 1922. By 1938 most people owned a wireless set, and Orson Welles' radio version of H G Wells' 'War of the Worlds' spread panic among listeners who believed that Martians had invaded Earth.*

Music Hall gave way *to the increasingly popular cinema; in 1933 horrified audiences were left gasping at the sight of Fay Wray in the clutches of the giant ape in the film 'King Kong'. By 1939, 20 million people went to the cinema every week.*

The world's first *television service was set up by Britain in 1936 - black and white, of course. Three years on there were 80,000 TV sets around the country, though programmes were discontinued the day war was declared.*

Commercial television *was introduced on 22nd September 1955, and Gibbs SR toothpaste were drawn out of the hat to become the first advert to be shown. Many believed adverts to be vulgar, however, and audiences were far less than had been hoped for.*

The Carnegie Library on Victoria Avenue opened a new junior library section in 1949. Little lads had knees in those postwar days. Dirty, scabby and knobbly, but they showed them off with pride. Rumpled socks, maybe, but they also dressed like little men. When did you last see a nine year old in a tie, jacket or short trousers? Ask yourself when did you last see a child of this age taking an interest in reading a book? This was over half a century ago when Enid Blyton books were not banned for lack of political correctness. The latest Biggles book

was eagerly grabbed from the bookshelf and their sisters loved to find out 'What Katy did next'. There were Boys' Own annuals and stories of the Secret Three having adventures in the dorm. Kids cannot be shifted from the computer screen or separated from their Gameboys now. The keen readers in the picture did not need their school to bring in literacy hour to make them read. They and their sisters wallowed in the printed word, losing themselves in a world of imagination conjured up by 'Coral Island' and 'Heidi'. As grandparents by now they must be approaching retiring age, wondering what happened to the bookshelves that homes used to have. It is all a time of CD racks. When these little chaps were pictured CD meant Charles Dickens. The modern youngster probably thinks he is some form of rap singer.

*B*right, cheerful delphiniums, red hot pokers wait to greet the visitors to Valley Gardens. The Royal Pump Room stands near the entrance. Perhaps the first step towards the gardens' creation was the realisation that 35 springs rise within the one acre of the Valley Gardens area. It was the discovery of the sulphur and mineral springs that brought people flocking to these grounds. The present layout of the gardens dates back to 1901 when they were enlarged. They remain popular, even though the heydays of the wells and springs have now long gone. The birth of the National Health Service in 1948 meant that the government could take over our welfare. There was no longer an attraction in taking the medicinal waters. Fortunately, the other delights of the gardens remain and continue to bring in locals and strangers alike to stroll happily in the sheltered dell along the side of a tinkling stream. Many a girl's heart has been won when her beau took her hand as they walked in the lovely surroundings of the floral displays. Young lovers and those recalling the tenderness of youth can be found on balmy summer evenings, finding enjoyment in each other's company. Romance might take a back seat if they stopped to remember that the centre of the gardens was once known as Bog Fields. This once marshy spot was the result of the many springs that surfaced in the area. Asking a sweetheart to take a walk in the Bog would not have the same ring to it as inviting her to promenade the gardens.

Bird's eye view

The aerial view of Harrogate, looking east, lets us see the balance that has been struck between building styles and open spaces. Montpellier Gardens and the edge of the Stray at West Park, with their carefully laid lawns and wooded sections, lend a rural feel to this part of town. The sweep of the buildings around the northern side of Prospect Square is a reminder of the excellence and taste of the late Victorian and Edwardian architect. Following the line of these buildings round and above the war memorial takes in the 1862 Wesley Chapel and Harrogate Theatre, the former Grand Opera House, built in 1900. The part of the town known as High Harrogate begins at the top of the picture, beyond the railway station. In early Victorian times there were two distinct parts to the town. They were, in effect, two separate villages, divided by a stretch of agricultural ground. High Harrogate is the older section. It was where the old highways met and hotels and inns were established there. It was also where the first mineral wells could be found. Modern Harrogate was formed when businessman Richard Ellis and the Carter brothers formed the Victoria Park Company to build houses, shops and hotels in an area that would link High and Low Harrogate. Builder George Dawson and the Bristol architect, JH Hirst, joined forces in producing some of the town's grandest structures. Parts of Parliament Street, the villas on West Park and Prospect Crescent stand as fine testaments to their imagination.

Looking at the town from this angle, the Ripon Road runs from left to right across the centre of the photograph as the A61 heads towards Killinghall. Most of the major halls, hotels and spa rooms can be seen. The Majestic Hotel, where Edward Elgar once stayed, is on the far right. During World War II the government requisitioned its

bedrooms. Harrogate was one of many such towns to which ministerial departments moved during wartime. These towns were seen as safer places to be than the big cities. The bombing raids were more likely to be centred on the industrial heartland of Britain, rather than leafy Harrogate. Someone else took refuge in a Harrogate hotel in 1926. In December, a countrywide search was

Memories of HARROGATE

undertaken to find Agatha Christie, the famous crime writer. Her abandoned car was found near her Surrey home. Newspapers speculated about the reason for her disappearance. Was it a failed love affair or a publicity stunt? Whilst it was probably a case of nervous exhaustion, the nation wondered for nearly 12 days. At last, she was discovered in the town's prestigious

Harrogate Hydro, now the Swan. She said that she had gone to London, seen a poster advertising Harrogate and just got on a train bound there on a whim. A chambermaid recognised her and alerted the authorities. Agatha's husband, Colonel Archie Christie, drove up north and collected her. The Swan, which dates from around 1700, is at the top centre of the photograph.

On one occasion - in 1911 - three queens were in the town at the same time - Queen Amelie of Portugal, Empress Marie of Russia and our own Queen Alexandra

The aerial view, taken in June 1955, shows the northern section of the town, with Ripon Road heading away from the war memorial towards its junction with Skipton Road. In the centre of the picture, on either side of the cross-roads, are the Royal Hall and Royal Baths Assembly Rooms. The former, on the Kings Road side, is now part of the Exhibition Halls and Conference Centre complex. Until 1939 the Royal Chalybeate Spa concert rooms and pleasure gardens, built by John Williams in 1835, stood near here. Across the way on Crescent Road, Baggaley and Briscoe had built the Royal Baths in 1897. The rich and famous flocked there to wallow in hot mud poultices and to drink what some described as 'that stinking brew' of sulphur water. Byron and Tennyson found inspiration for their poetry here and foreign royals patronised the waters regularly. On one occasion, in 1911, three queens were in town on the same day when Queen Amelie of Portugal, Empress Marie of Russia and our own Queen Alexandra (Edward VII's widow) came to visit. Those times of a century ago were great days for the spa town. Since the discovery of the first well in 1571, it had grown slowly. After the re-establishment of the monarchy in 1660, business developed. The first bathing house opened in High Harrogate in 1663. The wonder of the warm baths attracted such custom that there were 20 of them in place by the end of the 17th century.

Above: This was modern Britain even 40 years ago. In July 1961 rows of traffic jammed the roads leading past lines of uniform houses; the 'little boxes made of ticky-tacky' that folk singer Pete Seeger criticised. In Harrogate's defence, the little boxes were a bit more gracious than those on the estates that Mr Seeger sang about. Even so, they had a similar look to them. Neatly hedged front gardens, a garage and a back lawn meant that on a dark night you could easily mistake a neighbour's drive for your own. But it has been the traffic that has given the town its greatest headache in recent times. The A1 road, running some 10 miles east of the town, takes much of the long distance traffic away. But, travellers from York and Hull heading for the Dales or the Lake District head for Harrogate. Those coming north from Halifax, Keighley and Bradford make their way through here as well. That is before you even start to measure the volume of visitors to Harrogate itself. The town became a victim of its own position and success. A bypass opened in 1992, linking the York and Bradford roads, taking some traffic away, but it was nowhere near enough to make a significant effect. As the day is long, the bottleneck that is Harrogate centre remains clogged. Quadruple the cars and heavy lorries in this picture and you have an idea of the problem today.

Taken in June 1955, the pilot of the plane was looking east across the town towards High Harrogate. West Park, Parliament Street and Ripon Road that run north and south from the war memorial are the effective borders that separate Low from High Harrogate. In the foreground is the West Park edge of the large tract of open land known as the Stray. Protected from development by an act of Parliament, it represents Harrogate's determination to make the town an attractive place to live in and to visit. A large part of the town's budget is spent on the Stray and the gardens to keep them so. It is a healthy attitude that sets the town apart. There is no obvious profit in spending public money in such a way, but there are some things that money cannot buy. Serenity and a delightful environment are priceless. The Stray can trace its history back to the 1770 Act of Parliament that provided for the enclosure of the forest of Knaresborough. It is in the centre of this former wooded land that modern Harrogate stands. Realising the value of the medicinal springs to the town, it was decreed that 200 acres should stay unenclosed. The springs could be protected and the public had access to them. Until 1893 it remained as open pasture until the Corporation bought the grazing rights. It has cared for the cultivation and upkeep of the lawns for all our benefit ever since.

The railway line cuts across the middle of the view of High Harrogate, looking west with the cenotaph in the far distance. It was the coming of the railway that provided a kickstart to the town's growth. Until then it had enjoyed its reputation as a fashionable spa town, but one that was sleepily resting on its laurels. Rail travel changed that. In 1820 there was a population of just 4,000. With the coming of the Harrogate Improvement Act of 1841, the town's commissioners planned for its rapid growth. The railway arrived in 1848 and, with the opening of its new central station in 1862, tourists poured in. In addition, this tourism brought the establishment of many new businesses and residential quarters quickly developed.

The population doubled in the last two decades of the 19th century. Most of the town centre's grand buildings date from this late Victorian or Edwardian era. When this photograph was taken, on 17 October 1964, the great days of the spa had gone. European royalty no longer came to stay and the town had turned towards other outlets for its prosperity. Interested tourists still came to look at the various baths and pump rooms, but it was to the commercial sector that the town now looked. After World War II and with the coming of the NHS, the medicinal value of spa water declined. Amongst others, Bill Baxter, known as 'Mr Harrogate', decided that the way forward was to establish Harrogate as a conference and trade centre.

GETTING AWAY FROM IT ALL

Wartime petrol rationing *finally ended in May 1950. Fuel was affordable, hire purchase readily available, and car ownership began to increase. Self service filling stations began to open around the country during the 1960s, with petrol costing just over six shillings a gallon (30p).*

Britain's first stretch of *motorway was not, as is popularly believed, the M1. The eight-and-a-quarter miles long Preston Bypass - later part of the M6 - was opened by Prime Minister Harold Macmillan in December 1958.*

Vast swathes were cut *through the outskirts of towns as ring roads were built to take traffic away from town centres. The network of new motorways initially speeded the average journey, but by the 1970s huge holdups were a regular feature of motorway driving.*

Post-war prosperity *meant that more families could aspire to that badge of one-upmanship - a new car. Hot off the production line in 1959 was the Mini - destined to become the 1960s 'car of the decade'.*

The morning traffic wends its way up Parliament Street towards Leeds or Bradford in the south. West Park Stray is pictured to the right on this springtime day of 27 March 1962. It is already busy, but it was not always so. Before the 16th century, this was just a collection of small farming hamlets in the Knaresborough Forest. The forest is not a true description of what was here in those days. In the 14th century marauding Scots had burned down large areas of the once great forest, first referred to in documents in 1167. As small as it was, Knaresborough was the more important village. At the end of the 17th century it boasted 156 houses

to Harrogate's 57. There is no mention of Harrogate in the Domesday Book. Its name does not appear in print until 1332 when reference to it is made as part of the roll for Knaresborough Court. The place name of Harrogate comes from the Norse 'Here-gatte', meaning the way to the hill of the soldier. Many English towns have street names that include the word 'gate'. It means 'road' and not 'gate', as many think. The discovery of the mineral springs and their development saw Knaresborough pushed into the background. By 1800 the population of Harrogate had reached 1,000. Ten years later it had become 1,500, an increase of 50 per cent. After that, like Topsy, 'it just growed'. By the end of the 20th century there were an estimated 70,000 living in the town and more than double that number within the Harrogate District that includes Ripon, Pateley Bridge, Knaresborough and Masham amongst others.

E
ven in 1966 the town had come a long way from those far off times of the two little hamlets of High and Low Harrogate. In 1766 Tobias Smollett wrote that 'the water is celebrated for its efficacy in the scurvy and other distempers'. So it was, but times change. By the middle of the last century the town turned away from the spa waters for its prosperity and concentrated on other areas to bring in business. Harrogate became a conference and exhibition centre. In 1959 a temporary exhibition hall was created in the Spa Rooms Gardens. A few years later the toy industry was looking for a home for its trade fair. January was the traditional time of year that it exhibited in Manchester or Leeds. Having problems with venues in those cities, the industry turned to Harrogate for help. The Old Swan Hotel helped out by providing storage space for the manufacturers' and exhibitors' stock and the trade fair went ahead. It was a partnership that was to remain. Many of those living in the houses pictured on 29 May 1966 can thank the visionary leaders of Harrogate for their foresight in looking for different routes to prosperity for the town. By the end of the 20th century, temporary exhibitions had become permanent. In 1981 the International Conference Centre opened, linked with a large modern hotel. Political parties, trade unions, big business and all manner of delegates regularly hold exhibitions and conferences in the town. There were over 2000 events being held annually as the year 2000 began, bringing in £180 million to Harrogate's coffers.

Events & occasions

y 1934 the country was largely coming out of the darkest days of the depression. The corner had not been turned completely. There was still the Jarrow hunger march of 1936 to come. But, by and large, things were looking up. The summer had seen success on the sporting field. Fred Perry and Dorothy Round won Wimbledon titles; a British double that has never been repeated. Henry Cotton won the Open golf championship and our cricket team did not collapse as easily as it does today. The grand event at the showground on Wetherby Road was the annual Great Yorkshire Show. Huge marquees and grandstands dominated the arena for the event then as they do today. Show jumping competitions, exhibitions of livestock, ferret shows and all manner of country crafts were on display. Landowners, gamekeepers, farmers and poachers mixed merrily in the celebration of all that is best about rural England. Until 1951 (when it made Harrogate its permanent home) the Show was held in a different town around Yorkshire every year. For the thousands of visitors and spectators from the cities it was a chance to share in a way of life they had never known. Green wellies, brogues and hacking jackets, accompanied by the inevitable walking or shooting stick, appeared in countless numbers. In 1934 it was an age when crowds thrilled to hear the sound of the hunting horn as a pack of foxhounds entered the arena. The showground is also used for other events such as flower shows, but it is the Great Yorkshire Show that is the high spot on the calendar.

Majestic by name and majestic by nature, this fine hotel was ravaged by fire in 1924. Bystanders gathered to gaze horror struck as the flames leapt through the roof. The caps and bonnets of the watching crowd are typical of the period. Typical of any period is the fascination we have with fire. The Majestic was a fine building, but few in the crowd would have had any link with it. Yet, they stood and gawped, just as we would today. Happily, the fine band of firefighters was soon on the scene. The powerful fire engine would have been a far cry from the first one owned by the township. It was acquired for the princely sum of £120 in 1855 and then allowed to fall into disrepair. By 1861 it was unusable and two years later was reported to be lost. This early history reads

like a Whitehall farce. The machine was eventually found, but the engine and pump had been removed. By 1873 it had been put back together, but there was no horse to pull it. When one was acquired it was found to be blind in one eye! Fortunately, the professionalism of the service had improved for it to tackle this blaze. Restorations afterwards returned the hotel to its former glories and many distinguished visitors came to stay. The famous composer, Edward Elgar, of Enigma Variation fame, was here in 1927. His stay was marked by a plaque in the Valley Gardens. A walk in the gardens was named in honour of the great man. The hotel was damaged by fire once again, in September 1940. However, the Majestic once again overcame the problem and still flourishes on Ripon Road.

Below: On 31 January 1937 the market hall was destroyed by fire. The crane gantry was the place from which a precariously placed fireman had been hosing gallons of water into the flames. The power of the fire was too much for even the fictitious miracle workers of TV's Blue Watch on 'London's Burning'. The Harrogate firefighters tried their best, but the flames had too good a hold. These brave boys risked life and limb in trying to gain control, save property and prevent loss of life. The shiny fire appliance looks dated, compared with the monsters used today. They carry anything that could possibly be needed to cope with fires, toxic spillages and road crashes. In 1937 the basic turntable, water hoses and fire blankets were just about all that could be called upon. The fine clock tower largely escaped damage, but the main hall had to be rebuilt. The clock was a present to the town from Angela Burdett-Courts. A friend of the author Charles Dickens, she made the gift to mark her affection for the town that she often visited. Farrah's Harrogate toffee, advertised on the left, had been going since 1840. The shop on Royal Parade, where the toffee with its secret recipe was sold, closed in the mid 1990s. It was taken over by the proprietors of a chocolate shop across the road on Montpellier Parade. The Farrah name was kept and the shop continues to sell such mouth-watering delights as champagne truffles, peppermint cremes and caramel fudge. Yummy!

Bottom: This fire was not the first to strike the Market Hall. It had survived a previous one on 21 March 1914. Station Square was enlarged in the early 1950s and the market was enlarged. By the 1990s the building that was designed by Leonard Clarke was showing its age and, in 1991, was demolished. The Victoria Gardens Centre was built to replace it. The new shopping development covers 90,000 square feet. Its imposing central atrium has the malls to Cambridge Street and Market Place radiating from it. The first market hall was established in 1874. The idea of a popular market had first been proposed in 1841. In those days there was a host of barrow boys and hawkers blocking off the streets. However the first plans drawn up threatened to cut into parts of the Stray. Protesters objected violently. Mobs threw dead cats and eggs at those suggesting that the plans go ahead. Brass bands played their version of protest songs and the power of the people won the day. Pictured in 1937, fire officers and locals view the smoking ruins and twisted metal that wrecked the market. The very first building had been put up at a cost of £3,600. The latest centre to stand on this site cost £50 million. That is inflation for you.

A rms akimbo, this young woman in the foreground has had enough. The lads at the street party have been trying her patience. Cheeky boys have always been a pain. She had been slaving away baking buns, spreading sandwiches and pouring out ginger beer so that everyone could have a good time. Her friend in between the tables looks equally fed up. Now, come on ladies. Let your hair down a bit. Boys will be boys and they appreciate what you have done, deep down. They will show how much when they scoff the lot. Forced into clean shirts and ties for the day, they had to let off steam. The scene on Nydd Vale Terrace, in the very heart of Harrogate, was

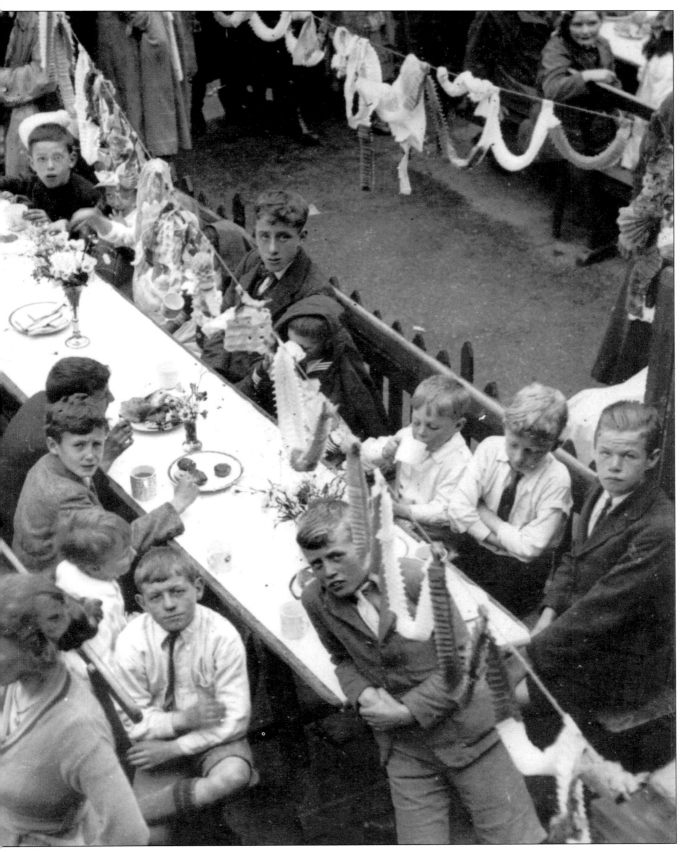

repeated up and down the country as celebrations were held to mark the end of the 1914-18 war. Benches were dragged out of church halls and trestle tables from schoolrooms and set out in the streets as the nation partied. Every effort was made to make sure it was a special occasion. Little table decorations and flower vases made sure that every-

thing was done properly and politely. Even the hungry children knew how to behave, once they had stopped playing up. They did not attack the grub until told to do so. Now, come on, ladies, put on a cheery face for the camera. It takes a thousand muscles to frown and only a handful to grin. You look so pretty when you smile.

Why is it that little lads have to get themselves on camera? Today, no outside TV broadcaster is safe from someone behind the subject of the shot trying to get his face seen. It was no different for the still photographer in 1919. The group in fancy dress could have done without the urchin in the gutter. If it had known he was there, then he would have been sent packing. As it was, the women of Mayfield Grove were ready to celebrate the end of the Great War. Soon, hubbies and sweethearts would be returning from the trenches and things could return to normal, for the lucky ones, that was. Too many had seen their loved ones left on some foreign field. But, you had to look forward.

The fancy dress they adopted for the street party showed the enterprise and skill of British womenfolk. Precious material had been raided and dresses adapted to create the cosmopolitan theme of the party. We can but admire the neat workmanship to create the shamrocks on the bonny Irish girl's dress and the clever creation of the little girl's kimono. Wales and Holland were also represented in the universal display. Just to keep things properly patriotic, God bless the lass wrapped in the union flag. All across the country scenes like this one were being repeated as the end of the hostilities was celebrated. The stitching and sewing of frocks and dresses could once again replace the manufacture of army uniforms and battledresses.

During the first world war the bond of the British Empire became stronger than ever. From the furthest corners of the map, they came to serve the cause. Heroes one and all, Aussies and Kiwis fell at Gallipoli, Canadians on Vimy Ridge and Indians at Gaza. Never had there been a time when those who acknowledged the British monarch as head of state felt such kinship. It was a bitter pill that it took carnage to bring togetherness. In memory of those from the Antipodes who were lost, 25 April was declared Anzac Day. It was on that date in 1915 that troops landed on Gallipoli to start a campaign that ended in a humiliating withdrawal the following December. Pictured on 7 June 1924, the boys from Australia have made a visit to the cenotaph to lay a wreath in honour of comrades who never returned. Harrogate folk turned out to share in the paying of respect. At the top left of the photograph is the Café Imperial. It was the height of elegance. Evening suited string quartets played an accompaniment to those sampling the exotic teas and aromatic coffees served there. Charles and Llewellyn Taylor made it the 'in' place to be. In 1962 it joined forces with Betty's Tea Rooms. Frederick Belmont, a Swiss confectioner, had come to England in about 1900. He loved the air and scenery of North Yorkshire as it reminded him of home. His first Betty's Café Tea Room opened on Cambridge Crescent in 1919.

Above: *It was on 21 January 1936 that Edward VIII was proclaimed King. The snow had fallen and the frost bit deep into the ground, as well as into the cheeks of the crowds gathered to hear the news. It was a matter of great public interest. The sailor King, George V, had led the monarchy through a war with his cousin, Kaiser Wilhelm. How much his subjects loved the man who had engineered the family name change from Saxe-Coburg-Gotha. Windsor was an English name and we applauded him for it. At his funeral, the following week, a lone piper would play the 'Skye boat song' as he went on his final voyage. Many of the crowd wore mourning in his memory. He would be missed. His had been the first royal voice the widespread public had really heard, thanks to the wireless. They took to his gruff voice and warmed to his plain speaking. 'I don't like abroad', he said, 'I've been there.' How we nodded sagely in agreement. But, it was a case of the king is dead, long live the king. Whilst wishing one monarch goodbye, it was time to welcome his successor. George's son was proclaimed Edward VIII and the onlookers forgot their sorrow and cheered the dawn of a new era. The 41 year old former Prince of Wales was young enough to be on the throne until the final quarter of the 20th century. Little did the watchers know that he would not see the year out.*

Right: *Gathered at the Municipal Buildings, with its back to the*

Crescent Gardens, the crowd listens intently to the proclamation of Edward VIII as King. His father had come to the throne in 1910 only because his elder brother, the Duke of Clarence, had died earlier. It was to be an irony that the next crowned British king would also be the second son. On another cold day in December of that year, this same crowd would listen to the king read out his abdication speech on the radio before slipping off into exile. He never made it to his coronation. Brought down by his love for a twice divorced American, whom the church and government could not accept, Edward VIII listened to advisers like Walter Monckton and prime minister Stanley Baldwin, but to no avail. He had been given the choice, the woman or the throne. He chose her. Those who came to listen to the proclamation in January could never have guessed that their new monarch had been carrying on an affair for four years. Gathered together, they listened with interest to the announcement and admired the splendour of the building from which it was read. What we know today as the centre for the Harrogate District of North Yorkshire was once the New Victoria Baths. It was built in 1871 as an addition to the Victoria Baths that had been the brainchild of John Williams. In 1832 he commissioned the architect John Clarke to design a single storey building with Ionic columns and classical lines. The New Victoria Baths changed to be the municipal offices in 1930.

The war memorial, known to all as the cenotaph, is the focal point of Prospect Square. So it should be. This fine obelisk, reaching 75 feet into the heavens, is a reminder of the ultimate sacrifice paid by those who fought in the defence of our beloved country. Veterans and youngsters stood side by side. A common bond joined profes-sional classes and labourers. Bullets and shells did not differentiate between victims. Each one who fell has rightly been afforded the same rank of respect on the roll of honour. The inscription now reads 'Our glorious dead 1914-1918. To all men and women who have given their lives in the service of their country in various hostilities since the second world war. We will

remember them'. This photograph was taken on 1st September 1923 at the unveiling of the cenotaph. At that time there was still hope that the losses felt in the Great War would act as lessons for future generations. It was a pious hope. Man's aggressive nature and greed would not protect him from the pain of war. It would all blow up again within a generation. How little we learn from our past mistakes. The 1914-18 war was supposed to help us build a land fit for heroes. Five years after it finished, the people were still waiting. The dark days of the depression were just around the corner. In the meantime, the large crowd that had come to honour the dead could focus on the imposing white structure and say a silent prayer.

Above: Representatives of all the services who performed so nobly in protecting our country provided the guard of honour for the unveiling of the cenotaph. The flags hung limply at half mast in honour of those who had fallen. You could have heard a pin drop as the presentation party approached the memorial. Wreaths were laid and prayers said. In the crowd many a quiet tear was shed for those who had died so that the rest could live in peace. The last post was sounded and every man, woman and child stood stiffly to attention. It was not a festival of celebration, but one of remembrance. Poppies, to recall the blood spilled in defence of the realm on the battlefields abroad, would be worn with pride each November in the future. Wreaths are still laid at war memorials throughout the country today, even though survivors of the 1914-18 war have long gone. It is important that each generation that comes along is reminded of the horror and futility of war, as well as remembering the bravery of those who fell. Gilbert Ledward designed the bronze panels on the Portland stone of the cenotaph. On them are inscriptions showing Britannia above a group of soldiers and a dove of peace flying over their heads. There is a scene of a call to arms and a list of the names of all those who perished. Lest we forget.

Above right: Just after 3.15 on a gloomy, wet September afternoon in 1923 the crowd had no thought of a warming cup of tea in the shelter of the Café Imperial. Hats firmly in place and brollies raised against the elements, Harrogate's inhabitants were thinking of those for whom a cuppa was no longer an option. It was to their memory that they had turned out. The better informed amongst the crowd might have started to ask a few questions after the ceremony was over. The war had been fought, so the politicians had said, to provide a better and safer life for all. Five years on and there was precious little sign of the improved housing conditions for the working classes. There were not enough jobs and working conditions were far from good. There was trouble in Europe, once again. The Germans were demonstrating fiercely against the crippling war charges put on them. The French occupation troops had fired on civilians and the German Chancellor had encouraged workers to go on strike. The country's currency was in ruins as the value of the mark crashed. At the start of the year it stood at 85,000 to the pound. By now, it had become 480 million. People wheeled the useless notes around in barrows. There was also talk that someone had been arrested in a beer hall in Munich for trying to stir up trouble with a new political party he had founded. He was a chap called Adolf Hitler. Remember the name, for it might crop up again in the future.

Memories of *HARROGATE*

Liveried footmen and uniformed outriders tell us that this is an important event. We all enjoy pageantry. Britain has its traditions. They should be defended fiercely. Dressing in grand robes and processing in carriages with highly polished coachwork make sure that the occasion is special. The passenger in the fine landau is the Lord Mayor of London. On 10 July 1939 Sir Frank Bowater had been specially invited to perform the official opening ceremony of the extension to the Royal Baths. The coach and four had been brought up from the capital, just for this occasion. A similar visit had been made in the early 1900s when an extension to the Royal Pump Room was opened. Sir Frank was able to see that the Royal Baths now included a greatly extended treatment block. The lounge hall was a beautiful sight. Its art deco elegance was a perfect backdrop to the pride of Harrogate. Unfortunately, the sound of mobilising troops across the Channel could be heard. Tanks would be rolling across Europe in less than two months' time. The world was about to change and the days of the town as a spa were to change with it. In 1947 there were 63,000 treatments. This compared with a figure twice as large 20 years before. The depression days of the 1930s had already taken their toll. The second world war would see Harrogate looking elsewhere than the mineral springs for business and future prosperity.

In front of the Bradford District Bank and the Lancashire and Yorkshire Bank people crane their necks to see what is happening. This part of Harrogate was the centre of important finance and business enterprises. Pictured is just one section of the huge crowd that gathered to witness the dedication of the town's war memorial. It seemed that every Harrogate resident had turned out to be part of the event. Thousand upon thousand ringed Prospect Square in 1923 as Princess Mary and Viscount Lascelles performed the unveiling ceremony. She was representing her father, George V. The Viscount lived at Goldsborough Hall and, later, at Harewood House. He took a particular interest in the affairs of the town. Unlike other visits when royalty was present, there were no flags being waved, no cheering subjects. The crowd was hushed to pay proper respect to

ROYAL WATCH

The talking point of the early 1930s was the affair of the Prince of Wales, later King Edward VIII, and American divorcee Wallis Simpson. Faced with a choice, Edward gave up his throne to marry her. His Nazi sympathies were kept strictly under wraps at the time.

By the end of World War II, the 19-year-old Princess Elizabeth and Lieutenant Philip Mountbatten RN were already in love. The couple's wedding on 20th November 1947 was a glittering occasion - the first royal pageantry since before the war.

King George VI's health had been causing problems since 1948, when he developed thrombosis. In 1951 the King - always a heavy smoker - became ill again, and he was found to be suffering from lung cancer. He died in the early hours of 6th February 1952.

Princess Margaret's announcement in 1960 that she was to wed photographer Antony Armstrong-Jones brought pleasure to many who had sympathised when she ended her relationship with Peter Townsend in 1955. Her marriage to Lord Snowdon itself ended in 1978.

the memory of the 841 brave men and women who had perished in the service of their country during the first world war. There was hardly a person watching whose life had not been touched by sadness. Whether it was a husband, a sister or a near neighbour, there was someone close who did not return. When the troops marched off nine years before, who could have guessed that their high hopes would soon be floundering in the Flanders mud? Each advance of a few yards cost hundreds of lives and some of those were being remembered on this day.

Above: Public health and cleansing became major topics of concern in the 20th century. The insanitary conditions of many Victorian homes and the lack of co-ordination of sewage disposal, rubbish clearance and the treatment of the sick was a national disgrace. Life expectation was short. Infant mortality was high. Only the well off seemed to prosper. The rich grew richer and the poor went under. Better education and more public spirited attitudes helped bring about the birth of the welfare state after the second world war. Harrogate's public health and cleansing services did not just respond to problems. They advised on food storage and how to protect it from infection. Different ways of packaging and wrapping were demonstrated. Shops were inspected to make sure that levels of hygiene were high. Vaccination programmes were launched to give our children a better chance of long life than that offered to earlier generations. Tuberculosis had been a major disease that struck down so many unfortunates. The public health service helped make it a rarity. Regular collections of household waste meant that the piles of stinking rubbish that our forefathers suffered were a thing of the past. The cleansing department made sure that it was not just a collection and disposal service. It was always on the lookout for salvage that could be recycled at a profit to the department. This would help keep the rates down. Collecting useful scrap was a lesson learned from wartime when bedsteads, pots and pans could be turned into aeroplanes.

Above right: The borough treasurer's department was responsible for mounting this display to inform the public how its money was being spent. Tradesmen and other creditors accounted for £1.7 million of the budget. This figure showed how costly it was to run a department that needed a large stack of goods and supplies so that it could function. Even over half a century ago, this was a huge amount. Wages to its employees accounted for another large slice. The 600 staff earned a total of £1,325 million. The average wage to the council employees was £2,200 per year, or £42 per week. As the national wage averaged out at about £15 per week, there must have been some high earners on the payroll. The town hall was always thought of as a growth industry. There was constant sniping at the huge administration costs of running the town and employing hordes of people to do jobs that could be done just as efficiently by fewer. This display tried to deflect that criticism. If the public did its sums properly, such information on show might have backfired. Those involved in public administration increased as the years went by. By 1991 there were 3,515 employed in this sector. Then came various nights of the long knives. By 1996 the numbers had been cut by nearly 40 per cent - down to 2,113 in service.

Below: This is a very orderly display. If the health department ran its affairs in 1959 as neatly as it set out its stall, then Harrogate residents were in safe hands. The main thrust was care of the young. In 1948 the Labour government had launched the NHS. Health minister Aneurin Bevan paved the way for cheap dental care, spectacles and medical treatment. For the young, old and unemployed much of the service was free. Antenatal clinics gave mums-to-be the chance to take part in exercise classes and receive advice about baby care. It had been the job of grannies to pass on tips to their daughters, but we were coming to a period when families moved around more. It was less common to find relatives living in the same street as used to happen. Running relaxation classes and giving guidance on bathing and feeding became part and parcel of the midwife's job. Care continued after the birth. Visits were made to make sure that the baby was thriving. Sight and hearing tests were given and regular weight checks made. As the child grew to be of school age, the health department followed across the school threshold. Free milk and subsidised meals were provided. Nitty Nora, as the school nurse was unkindly known, checked for head lice on a regular basis. Shame fell on the family that had to use that special bottle of foul shampoo to get rid of the nits.

Bottom: Water has been Harrogate's blood, its flow of life. New reservoirs were built in the 20th century to cater for its basic needs as residents used up a staggering 35 gallons a day for every man, woman and child. Roundhill reservoir at Masham was begun in 1903. When completed, in 1912, it had cost £500,000, but had a capacity of 525 million, supplying 3.5 million gallons a day. It also served the needs of Knaresborough, as its own reservoir was antiquated. As well as a council department to deal with the public water supply, there was also a Wells and Baths section with responsibility for the town's famous medicinal waters. A former chairman of this committee, Francis Barber, wanted to develop the spa even further. In 1928 he issued far reaching plans for a 'cure park'. This meant turning the centre of Harrogate into one where all the facilities of a modern spa could be found. Visitors would have to pay a fee to pass through toll barriers that would encircle the centre. These fees were to fund even more improvements. A forum would be built on Crescent Gardens and council officers and officials moved to a remodelled New Victoria Baths. Between Swan Road and Crescent Gardens there would be a new assembly hall. It was too much for the council to bear, though it did take on some of the suggestions. Although the Wells and Baths Department continued to play a part in council affairs, by the time of this exhibition its influence was minimal. The great days of the mineral water treatments, massages and mud baths had gone.

Left: Jolly bunting, flapping in the breeze; this back street scene is almost timeless. All over the country this sight appeared at various times in the 20th century. It happened whenever there was something of national importance to celebrate. Then, it was time to party. The last occasion we have seen such scenes was in 1981, when the Prince of Wales married the sadly missed Diana Spencer. Coronations, jubilees and weddings have all given the British the chance to share the gaiety together. This photograph was taken in 1919 and the celebrations about to begin were born of hope and relief, rather than joy. There had been four long years of hostilities that were supposed to be all over by Christmas. Just because a grand duke in far off Sarajevo had been assassinated, the country was plunged into the bloodiest conflict the world had ever seen. Little wonder that we were glad it was all over. The street is empty, but soon will be filled with raucous laughter and the shouts of excited children. At the moment the mums are indoors producing jellies, ice creams, old fashioned lemonade and sandwiches. Wiping their hands on their pinnies, the women baked and baked, sharing the load with neighbours, to produce a feast fit for a king. 'Can I lick the bowl, mum?' was a common request from the children as the cake mixes were turned out into the baking tins. 'Just this once' really meant 'until next time'.

Below: Fly the flag and cheer loudly. Royalty was in town and we were all thrilled to see her. The crowd, enjoying the autumn sun, fell quiet as the special guest stepped forward to make the dedication. The loudspeakers carried her words across the stilled air. It is 17 September 1932. Mary, the Princess Royal, was representing her father, George V, at the official opening of Harrogate General Hospital on Knaresborough Road. The 35 year old princess was the only daughter amongst the 6 children that Queen Mary bore her husband. The Princess Royal had good connections in the Harrogate district. She was married to the Earl of Harewood. The building gave good service until a newer programme of hospital building took place in the mid 1970s. The new District Hospital, close by on Lancaster Park Road, opened its doors for the first time in January 1975. Another royal princess came along to perform the ceremony. This time it was the turn of Princess Mary's niece, Princess Margaret. Patients were transferred in stages to the new hospital and the importance of the General Hospital gradually declined. It was demolished in the late 1990s. No sign of it remains. In its place is a new Crest housing estate. Home owners of the future will not realise that they are treading the path that countless numbers of caring doctors and nurses trod for much of the last century.

At work

A new storage reservoir for the famous spa waters, built in 1867, enabled it to be accessible all year round

Convalescence needs many things for success. Skilled doctors, caring nurses and careful treatment are musts. A bit of sunshine does no harm, either. These two patients have been brought out to enjoy the sun's rays. It is amazing how much better we all feel with just a little bit of sun on our backs. In these ladies' cases, the sun was on their fronts. There were several hospitals and convalescent centres around Harrogate at one time. One of the best known was Bath Hospital, later the Royal Bath Hospital. This could easily have been a scene typical of the care it offered. Opened in 1826 on land donated by the Earl of Harewood, it relied on contributions from visitors for much of its funding. By the middle of the century these were running at over £1,000 per annum. It only opened for part of each year to deal mainly with those who were visiting the town and the local needy. This gave the poorer members of the community a chance to use the healing powers of the spa waters. However, the new storage reservoir for Bogs Field sulphur water enabled the hospital to stay open all year round from 1867 onwards. Then it had 40 beds. This rose to 150 in the 1880s when the hospital was rebuilt. The hospital officially reopened in 1889. A convalescent wing was added at a cost of £50,000. It became known as the Royal Bath and Rawson Convalescent Home, one of its main benefactors being Elizabeth Rawson. Closure came its way in 1994.

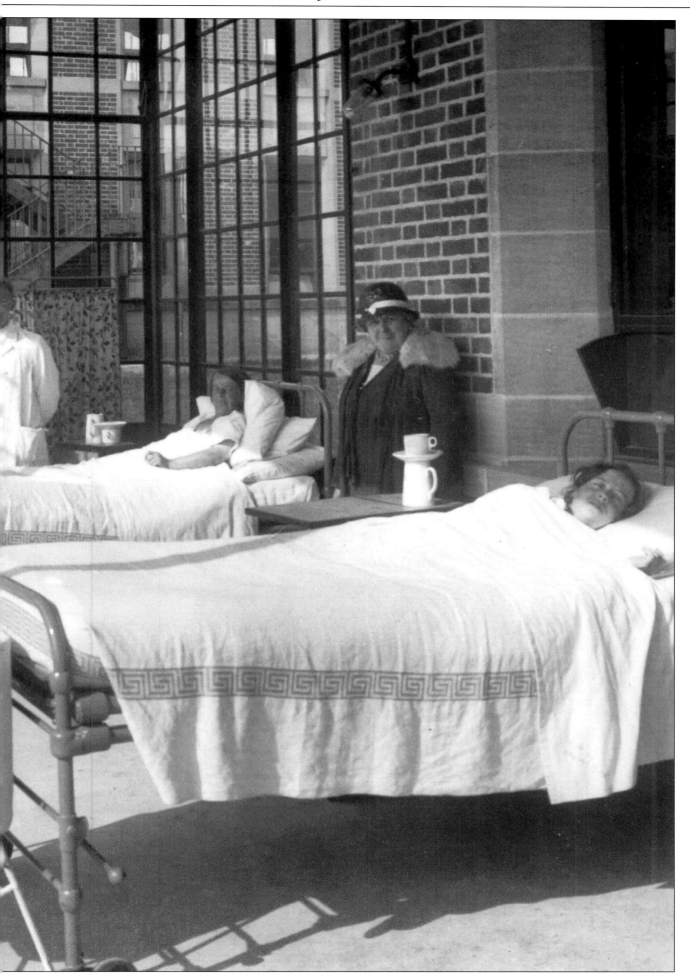

Y ou could be forgiven for thinking that this is the framework for the town's rival to Blackpool's Big Dipper. The planks at the top look a lot like the tracks for the centrepiece of an amusement park. But, it is no such thing. It is just the style of scaffolding that was used in 1927. Pictured on 8 July, health and safety would have a field day in the 21st century with this scene. Although there is some boarding at pedestrian level, the lack of warnings signs, the state of the guard rails and the ease with which a youngster could get on to the site would raise more than an eyebrow today. We live in a nanny state. In those far off days, if you were daft enough to put yourself in danger, that was your lookout. The scaffolding is around the rebuilding work on the Yorkshire Penny Bank. Situated on James Street, the General Post Office had occupied this site in earlier days, when the site cost £11,000. The work taking place when this scene was photographed would cost £25,000. Nicholsons of Leeds undertook it, to a design by the architects Chorley, Gibbon and Foggett, also of Leeds. Banking in the late 1920s was more a matter of pennies than pounds, so the bank was well named. The dark days of the depression were beginning. Work was hard to get. People had to tighten their belts and there was little spare cash for investment or savings. In later times, the building became the York City County Bank.

Below: At first glance this could be the skeleton of any building and for any purpose. The box girders and super-structure resemble the bones of a whale from some museum of natural history. Certainly, it is going to be a large structure. A clue as to its eventual use can be gained from the banked sweep of the struts and spars in the centre. It is to be a cinema. Soon, seating will be placed on the supports and a further source of entertainment will be on hand for the citizens of Harrogate. This will be the Regal, built in 1937. When it opened many a cuddling liaison took place on its back seats. Packets of Payne's Poppets would be passed round. Couples indulging in over energetic fumbling would have the usherette's torch pointed at them. Young lasses, when watching the film, would swoon over the dark, good looks of Errol Flynn as he swashbuckled his way through 'The Charge of the Light Brigade' and 'The Adventures of Robin Hood'. The lads would try to identify with those tough guys of the screen, Edward G Robinson and Jimmy Cagney. Talking out of the corner of their mouths like Edward G in 'Little Caesar' or admiring Cagney's role in

'Angels with dirty faces' the American influence affected Harrogate's young bucks. Cries of 'you dirty rat' had their roots in the magic of Hollywood gangsters rather than in pest control. Such remarks were often hurled at the man operating the cine-projector when it broke down in the middle of an exciting part.

Bottom: The building of the Regal Cinema was well under way when this photograph was taken. It opened on 18 September 1937. On that memorable Saturday evening 'Glamorous Nights' was the main feature. This Otto Kruger/Mary Ellis film was not the only attraction. In those days you got better value for money. There was usually a 'B' movie to sit through, as well. The second feature may not have been much good, but it provided a breeding ground for new actors. Where would the future president of USA, Ronald Reagan, have been without them? 'That's all folks' from Fred Quimby and the Hanna-Barbera characters Tom and Jerry entertained us in cartoons throughout the 1940s and beyond. There was the important Pathé News slot. With

no television for us, these newsreels brought pictures and stories from around the world that we had never witnessed before. The Regal possessed a mighty Compton organ, which was a popular attraction. It was a grand cinema with seating for 494 in the circle area alone and a total capacity of 1,600. Built on the site of the old 1865 St Peter's School, it was later called the ABC. It converted to a twin screen format in 1973. Eventually, the stalls were converted into a pub, the Dalesman. Falling audiences rang its death knell. Glenda Jackson, the Oscar winner who was to become a Labour MP, starred with the rumbustious Oliver Reed in 'Triple Echo' in the last film to be shown on the single screen. The last ones on the twin screen were 'First Blood' and 'ET'. Reidy & Co of Bradford demolished the memories of a large crowd of onlookers as well as the cinema in August 1983.

Above: Traps and poisons are displayed to highlight the dangers of the unwanted guest, the rat. The main display is headed 'rodent control'. Even in 1959, the first moves towards classier titles were being suggested. We used to have the rat catcher, but he became the official rodent operative. There was an important message being put over in the Royal Hall. Casual attitudes towards hygiene had caused illness and disease to be of concern to the health service. The NHS was still in its infancy, having come into being just over a decade before. The state took its responsibility very seriously. It had a duty to educate the public as well as offering treatments and cures. Prevention was better than trying to put things right after the event. Mass immunisation programmes, particularly against polio and smallpox, were instituted. Councils were encouraged to act against air pollution, a major cause of chest complaints. Various clean air acts, highlighted on the left of this display, meant that smokeless zones were introduced. People had to burn different fuel and factories had to control the burning of their waste through belching chimneys. Older readers will remember those days in the middle of the 20th century when large towns and cities were covered in a pall of smoke. Wintertime smog saw people walking along wearing masks and coughing as the poisonous fumes crept into their lungs. Even the smaller towns where heavy industry was not a problem had its share of the foul air. Dirty collars and cuffs and specks of dirt on shirtsleeves meant that a blouse did not last long before it went into the wash.

Below centre: Back in 1818, Thomas Telford, the pioneering engineer of the industrial revolution, suggested linking the canals with rail tracks to help the linen trade move its goods more easily. At that time the tracks would use horse drawn trucks and access to the port of Hull would be made easier. Although the idea was not properly taken up, it was not forgotten. When the linen trade revived in the 1840s it coincided with the mania for steam locomotives. The first line to Harrogate was from the York and North Midland branch in 1848. The formation of the NER in 1854 led to greater expansion. The 1859 Act of Parliament allowed Harrogate branches to be built. The station that celebrated its centenary in this photograph opened in 1862. Within a further three years there was a regular service to Bradford, operating 10 trains per day. Leeds was only 45 minutes away and the London service established a connection in just over six hours by 1870. The days of horse drawn coaches thundering along the turnpikes to Darlington and Normanton were numbered. The age of steam and, eventually, 'anoraks' had arrived. The spa town of Harrogate was in easy reach of the rest of the country. Its popularity increased dramatically as the influence of the iron horse spread. In the photograph, behind the centenary stand, is an advert for John Farrah's special toffee. How many ounces of that succulent mixture, first manufactured in 1840, have been sucked and crunched on rail journeys over the years?

The Royal Pump Room was built in 1842 at a cost of £3,000 to a design created by Isaac Shutt. It covered the strongest sulphur well in the world. For some it was too strong. In 1697 Celia Fiennes called it 'so strong and offensive I could not force my horse near'. During the 17th and 18th centuries remarkable cures for a variety of diseases were recorded. Word spread and invalids and hypochondriacs jostled with the able bodied to seek preventions and cures. The wares were supposed to be particularly good in the treatment of malaria, TB and bronchitis. At its peak, there were over 250,000 visitors each year. Many had come at the express wish of their doctors. They recognised that the mineral springs had a beneficial effect. Before the pump house was built there had been a cupola supported by pillars erected over the spring. Erected there in 1806, it was taken to Tewit Well on the Stray when the Royal Pump Room was built. An outside pump to provide free sulphur water for the general public to 'enjoy' was placed outside the building. The vacuum pumps inside drew water from the well in the basement. When they were added the need for well-women to draw the water disappeared. One of the last of these was Betty Lupton, known as the 'queen of the well'. Visitors drank the water in the pursuit of health and happiness. The Royal Pump Room is now a museum.

Bettys & Taylors of Harrogate - a special blend of taste and service

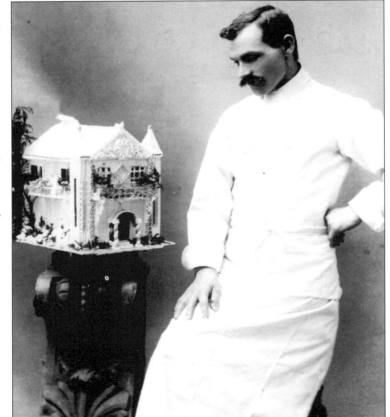

That Harrogate became the tea drinking 'capital' of Britain - and still is today - is due very much to the extraordinary efforts of two families, one Swiss and one Yorkshire.

Born in York, in 1866, Charles Edward Taylor owed his career in the tea trade to his elder brother, Llewellyn. Through family Quaker connections, Llewellyn had secured an apprenticeship with the London tea and coffee firm of James Ashby, and by his early 20s had made a name for himself buying tea and coffee for Ashby's customers in the North East. He persuaded the Ashby family to give his younger brother Charles a sales job, building - from scratch - a customer base in the South West. This involved getting to know not just the local grocers in the area, but also their local water, so that he could buy specific teas in the London Auction and create blends which grocers would promote as their own 'house blend, specially suited to the local water'.

Charles lost his job within the year; not because he was a failure at selling, but because he was headstrong about the teas he wanted Ashbys to buy for the new South West clientele. He took a few risks in buying teas he thought would suit his potential customers, and one particular purchase was regarded by the Ashbys as a risk too far. Charles offered to pay for the tea personally, but in the ensuing disagreement lost his job. One could imagine that Llewellyn would have been mortified to be let down by his younger brother, but he wasn't. Coming from a strong Quaker background, Llewellyn had faith in his brother, and offered to lend Charles the money to set up as a tea and coffee merchant in his own right.

Charles' father William, a well connected travelling salesman in the West Riding working for a Liverpool dried fruit merchant, suggested he base his new business in Leeds where he, William, could introduce and recommend him to all the best grocers in the West Riding. And so C. E. Taylor & Co. was formed, in 1886, operating from a small warehouse at 14 Basinghall Street in Leeds.

Top left: *Charles Taylor pictured to commemorate the 50th anniversary of the founding of the company in 1886. He lived in Harrogate from 1896 until his death in 1942.* ***Above centre:*** *Frederick Belmont pictured with one of his confectionery masterpieces, circa 1904.*

The Grove in Ilkley. At the 'Kiosks', coffee was roasted daily in the window with the aroma drifting out into the street to tempt in passers by. Exotic tea blends were sold including a House Blend particularly suited to the local waters. At the back of each shop was a tasting room where customers could try before they bought. It was but a short step to convert these tasting rooms into simple cafés. The Kiosk Cafés were very much like the old London Coffee Houses of two centuries earlier, places for business men, lawyers, accountants, bankers and merchants to meet to trade, gossip or play chess and dominoes. Simple 'no-nonsense' luncheons were served as morning coffee spilled over into lunch time. A further Kiosk was opened, in Wakefield, in 1898.

In the face of stiff local competition Charles struggled to build his business, even with his father's recommendations, until he realised the potential of the fast growing Yorkshire spa towns of Harrogate and Ilkley. Now full of guest houses, hydros and hotels there was a strong demand for a local supply of freshly roasted coffee. In 1895 Charles opened 'Kiosk' shops at No. 11 Parliament Street in Harrogate and No. 32

Above left: *Taylors Tea House, in the Bog Valley Gardens, providing a welcome antidote for visitors taking the waters, pictured in 1906.* ***Top:*** *A picture taken in 1901 of Taylors 'Kiosk' Café in Parliament Street, the haunt of businessmen from 1895 until its closure in 1963.*

Seeing even greater potential for catering in Harrogate, Charles won the municipal catering contract for the Valley Gardens Tea House, The Winter Gardens at the Royal Baths, and the Royal Spa Concert Rooms.

The success of catering for more ladylike clientele at the Spa inspired Charles to open two much more genteel lady-friendly cafés, The Café Imperial in the Grove, llkley in 1900, and in 1905 his jewel in the crown, The Café Imperial, in the imposing Scottish baronial-style building in Harrogate's most prominent site at No 1 Parliament Street.

The Café Imperial in Harrogate served morning coffees, afternoon teas and luncheons, with a 'clubby' smoke room in the basement, an elegant first floor luncheon room, non smokers' room and various function rooms for weddings and children's parties on the upper floors. The fifth floor party room housed the mechanism for the magnificent clock built by William Potts of Leeds, by which all the town centre businesses set their lunch and tea breaks.

*Above: "They came to take our waters; they much prefer our tea!" the Taylors slogan ran. Visitors recovering from the Harrogate Sulphur Water with a cup of Taylors tea, in 1906. **Right:** Taylors Café Imperial, the Scottish baronial-style building which still dominates the Harrogate skyline.*

The growth and prosperity of C. E. Taylor was disrupted by the upheaval of the Great War. By the time Charles, and Llewellyn's sons Bernard and Douglas came back from the war to join the business, fresh competition was about to appear in Harrogate - fresh from Switzerland.

Frederick Belmont, born in 1883, had no family to help him get started in life. His mother died while he was a baby and his father, a miller near Bern in Switzerland, had died trying to rescue his youngest child from a mill fire. Now orphaned, he was brought up in foster homes. He was a headstrong boy, always in trouble at school, but he was determined to get on in life, and trained first as a baker. Then, as he realised where his great talent lay, he trained further as a confectioner and chocolatier.

In 1907 he came to England to seek his fortune. It was what many a Swiss lad was doing at the time, and he followed in the footsteps of the likes of Cesar Ritz, the son of an alpine goatherd who founded the Ritz Hotel in London.

Left: *The first Bettys, opened in 1919, just across the road from their great rival the Café Imperial (just visible to the left).* ***Below:*** *The Starbeck Bakery's pastry bakehouse, 1926, still in operation in 2000.*

London was a big place for a provincial Swiss boy who couldn't speak a word of English and quite unintentionally Frederick boarded a train heading for Yorkshire. He alighted at Wakefield... and never went back. He had a succession of jobs over the next few years, sometimes with Swiss confectioners already established in Yorkshire, sometimes as a consultant to businesses like Farrah's Harrogate who wanted to learn how to make chocolates and confectionery the proper continental way. It was in Harrogate he finally settled in 1910. The pure sweet air reminded him of his native Alps...and his landlady's daughter, Clare, was rather sweet too! Frederick and Clare married in 1917. Clare's widowed aunt, Mary Wood, put up the money for them to start their own business - 'Bettys', a continental-style Tea Room and patisserie in Cambridge Crescent, right in the centre of Harrogate, opposite Taylors Café Imperial. Frederick was convinced that his combination of mouth-watering Swiss confectionery, an elegant continental 'fresh and dainty' ambience with musicians playing and fresh flowers everywhere, together with his wife's Yorkshire warmth and hospitality would be a recipe for success. It was, and soon he was writing home to his sister in Switzerland, proudly telling her of princesses and admirals taking tea at Bettys. 'Under Royal and Distinguished Patronage' proclaimed Bettys' note paper! Building on success, Frederick opened three further Tea Rooms during the 1920s and 30s, together with a bakery in Starbeck, which produced all the bread, cakes, pastries and chocolates.

Top: *Bettys staff outing to Windermere in 1931. In the centre are Mr and Mrs Belmont.*
Left: *A Bettys advert from the 1920s promoting Music at Bettys.*

As the business grew, Frederick needed to rely more and more on others to uphold his meticulous Swiss standards. Three devoted local girls emerged as his lieutenants, each of whom served him for more than fifty years. There was the formidable Miss May Carter who ran the Harrogate Café, the charming Miss 'Waddie' Waddington who ran the Harrogate shop, and Jessie Radcliffe who kept order at the Starbeck bakery - no mean feat with several lively young Swiss confectioners on the staff! These three joined Bettys straight from school; 'Waddie' in 1919, May in 1922 and Jessie, in the very week in 1926 when Agatha Christie went missing in Harrogate. Jessie was only taken on for two weeks temporary work, but she was still hard at work at Bettys in 1977, when, as the high spot of her long career, she personally delivered a magnificent Royal Jubilee Cake to Buckingham Palace.

By the 1930s both the Belmont and Taylor families were facing crises of succession; they were very short of heirs! Frederick and Clare Belmont had no children, nor had the two second generation Taylor boys, Bernard and Douglas. Both families looked for nephews. Bernard Taylor had a nephew on his wife's side, Francis 'Jim' Raleigh, a teenager anxious to find a settled home, as his mother was a touring Shakespearean actress with no base.

Frederick Belmont had a nephew in St Gallen in Switzerland; his sister was struggling financially to bring up her three children, amongst them 13 year old Victor Wild.

Left: *Two of Bettys adverts from the 1930s.*
Below: *The glamorous girl on the right is Jessie Radcliffe, who joined Bettys in September 1926, the week Agatha Christie went missing, and stayed for 55 years until her retirement in 1981. Mr Belmont called her "Chessie".*

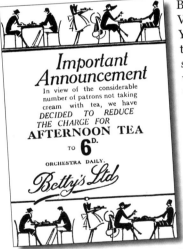

Important Announcement In view of the considerable number of patrons not taking cream with tea, we have DECIDED TO REDUCE THE CHARGE FOR **AFTERNOON TEA** TO **6** D. ORCHESTRA DAILY. *Betty's Ltd*

Both boys, Jim and Victor, came to Yorkshire and joined their family businesses, starting at the bottom with a view to proving themselves worthy successors.

Both were sent to London for additional training. Jim followed the family tradition and studied tea and coffee tasting with Ashby's. Frederick wanted Victor to train in the kitchens of one of the great hotels, and he interviewed the Head Chefs at the Ritz, Savoy and Claridges, before deciding that Claridges was going to have the privilege of training his nephew!

The young men returned to Yorkshire and put their training into practice under the eagle eyes of their families. Their opportunity to take on the leadership of their respective family businesses came in the difficult years following the second world war.

Right: Jim Raleigh (left) and Victor Wild taken in 1994. After Taylors joined Bettys in 1962, Jim stayed on as tea and coffee buyer, and consultant for thirty more years, until 1994. Top: Bettys, 1922. All laid up for a Wedding Breakfast. Above: Bettys advert 1930s: Important Announcement.

Frederick Belmont died in 1952, and Victor Wild became Managing Director of Bettys; Bernard Taylor died in 1956 and Jim Raleigh became Managing Director of Taylors.

Both businesses had struggled through the war, and the ensuing years of rationing and austerity, and both could easily have given up. In the end it was the Taylors who decided to sell. Jim had no children of his own and there was no other family member interested in running the business. Victor, on the other hand, had children and as the younger man, still had the determination to prove that he had his uncle's creative talent and the business acumen to lead Bettys through difficult times. So, in 1962, Bettys bought Taylors, and the company that was to become known as 'Bettys & Taylors of Harrogate' was born.

The little tea and coffee importing business in Leeds was moved to Harrogate by Victor Wild in 1971 and in an extraordinary leap of faith he set about turning the clock back to those early Taylor days, to the craft of blending tea to suit local water. 'Yorkshire Tea' was the result. It is a name which conceals a secret: there is more than one Yorkshire Tea! Slightly different versions of Yorkshire Tea are produced to suit different local waters. Originally conceived as teas to suit just Yorkshire's water variations - between the soft Pennine waters of the west, the hard borehole waters of the east, and the 'grid' mixtures of the south - Yorkshire Teas are now demanded everywhere, not least by the people of South West England, where Charles Taylor did his pioneering work over a century ago!

Now run by the third generation of that Swiss, but now very Yorkshire, family, Bettys and Taylors of Harrogate's present success owes everything to past traditions.

Frederick Belmont's Bakery, his pride and joy, is still the creative heart of the business, where traditional Yorkshire and Swiss craft techniques, which have been abandoned by most, are practised by a team of sixty skilled bakers, confectioners and chocolatiers

Bettys - the curious blend of continental café and archetypal English tea room - still flourishes, now in Harrogate, York, Ilkley and Northallerton. The two Taylors 'Café Imperials' in Ilkley and Harrogate were renamed 'Bettys' thirty years ago.

This kind of old fashioned attention to detail and quality has led to Taylors of Harrogate having an international reputation as one of the best tea and coffee specialists in the world, with exports to the Americas, Japan and Australia as well as much of Europe.

...and all this was started by two ordinary but very gifted young men who you wouldn't have thought would have stood the slightest chance of turning their creativity and craftsmanship into business success.

Harrogate wouldn't have been the same without them.

Above: Yorkshire Tea and Yorkshire Fat Rascals. Two of Bettys and Taylors most famous products. Below: Bettys today: Frederick Belmont would be proud to see his dreams still thriving three generations later.

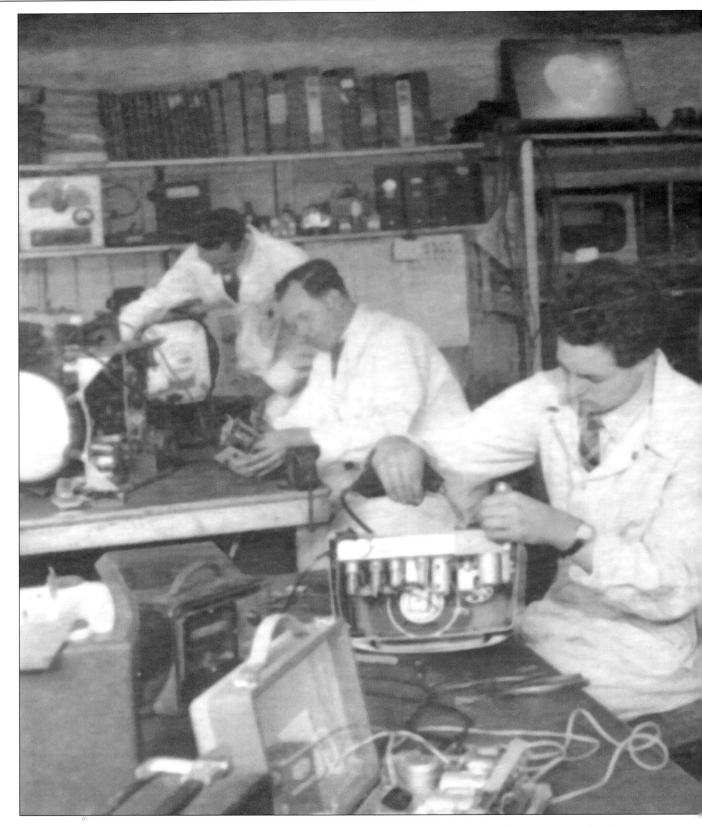

It was a busy old time in April 1957 in the workshop of Topham Bros television and radio workshop. Five of the large workforce, Karl Horner, Gordon Green, David Patill, Dennis Wright and Jack Donegan were all skilled technicians. They had learnt their trade and cut their eye teeth on the valves and circuits of the old wireless. No home in the country could exist without one. In the 1950s, weaned on such comedy greats as Tommy Handley in

ITMA, we gathered round the radio to chuckle at the hilarious antics and quickfire humour of Arthur Askey. His 'Hello Playmates', scripted by Denis Goodwin and Bob Monkhouse, was hugely popular. The 'left hand down a bit' of 'The Navy Lark', the zany cracks of the Goons and the cheeky chappie, Max Miller, amused millions. Whilst working to repair the sets, the Topham Bros staff were entertained by 'Workers' Playtime' coming over the tannoy. Popular singers and enter-

THE BUST TO BOOM YEARS

The country was in a bad way at the end of the war in 1945. Nazi bombs had destroyed railways, docks, factories and mills, and hundreds of homes lay in ruins. Britain had to borrow heavily - which meant increasing exports by 75 per cent.

During the war, car factories were given over to producing tanks, aircraft and munitions. Car production resumed in 1945, but as fast as they came off the production line, new vehicles were being exported and few went on sale in Britain.

By the 1950s British economy was back on track. At its worst, unemployment reached only around 400,000. Ordinary working people could afford to buy the latest kitchen equipment, televisions - and a family car.

During the Swinging Sixties more people had money to spend, and Britain was on track to becoming a consumer society. Foreign holidays gained in popularity, and Spain became a firm favourite. In 1968 you could book a Sky Tours package holiday in Benidorm for around 36 guineas.

tainers of the day often appeared on that show. But, it was a period of change. Televisions began to appear in the better off homes and were soon to be standard equipment in every house. The BBC had been threatened by the introduction of ITV in 1955. It tried to spike the new channel's guns by putting the 'Donald Duck Story' on TV. However, it was the killing off of Grace Archer in the radio soap 'The Archers' that stole the show. The technicians at Topham's transferred their radio skills to the new media. Bush and Pye television screens and cabinets appeared on the workbench just as often as broken radios.

WATER WORKS

A simple display of the way in which the domestic water supply works was interesting to those who did not have a clue about plumbing. To many, the hot water cistern was just a mystery that worked well, so why bother understanding it? The central display gave us more of an idea of how the overall water scheme operated. Helped by models and written descriptions, visitors were able understand how it all came together. It is one of the most important utilities that we have. After all, it is one of only two to be found on a Monopoly board! There is quite a history behind the development of the town's water works. In 1846 the Harrogate Waterworks company took over the town supply. It encouraged the passing of an 1869 Act of Parliament that allowed it to build a series of works and reservoirs to meet the growing needs of the population. Haverah Park, Harlow Hill and the 30 million gallon Ten Acres reservoir were all earmarked as sites for development. Even with these additions, the growth in population in the late 19th century saw demand far exceed supply. Shortages were particularly acute in summer. Two Beaver Dyke reservoirs, holding 147 million gallons, and the Scargill reservoir with its 129 million gallon capacity helped ease the problem. In 1897, the Corporation bought out the company for £205,000 and took over its administration. When asked for a glass of lemonade, mums could now tell the children to drink Corporation pop.

Above: Harrogate Corporation was proud of its achievements and the central display showed a model of the town and outlying districts. Around and above it were various charts and tables listing an outline of works completed and those in production. Much was made of the way the public had been served and the benefits it got from such an efficient body. At the tail end of the 19th century the Corporation had taken over the running of a new electric utility company. Other companies were interested in supplying the town's electricity, but Councillor David Simpson, a farseeing man, urged the Corporation to take control of the work for itself. He had seen the trouble caused by private gas and water companies in the past. Not responsible to the Corporation, they had been more interested in quick profit than public service. Roads were dug up willy-nilly without any consideration for others. Cynics amongst those reading this might wonder about what is new! Local candlemakers were against the idea as they could see their livelihood being threatened. Some of the council members also pooh-poohed the idea. The mayor, Charles Fortune, was against the idea. He felt it was too risky a venture for the Corporation. Many hotels were lit by gas and would not wish to switch to electricity. Despite the objections, the municipal electric works were built on the Corporation's irrigation farm system in 1897. Councillor Simpson was proved right. Demand grew and electricity became profitable for both the Corporation and its townspeople.

Top: The Royal Hall was not just a theatre. It was also an assembly room and exhibition centre. Before the coming of the Harrogate National Conference and Exhibition Centre in 1981, the Royal Hall, or Kursaal as it was once called, was the focus for many displays and exhibitions. This one was mounted by Harrogate Council to show off its work in the community and pass on valuable messages to the general public. Public health was the thrust of this section. The development of the refuse vehicles over the preceding 50 years made interesting viewing. From the horse drawn carts of the 1920s through to the tipper style of vehicle, the aim was the same. Get the rubbish from home to tip as quickly and as efficiently as possible. Harrogate Council used the language of the polite. Dustbin wagons were named refuse vehicles. Perhaps the dustbin men were refuse disposal operatives. Also on display was a section simply entitled 'food'. Here, visitors were asked to think about their diets. The last remnants of wartime rationing had gone. We were in a time of Harold Macmillan's 'never had it so good'. Even in 1959 the benefits of eating sensibly were recognised. It is not just a current fad. School milk was on the agenda for every primary school youngster and housewives were asked to supply families with a good mix of fresh fruit and healthy fish. Too much red meat was discouraged, even then. It was not an easy message to get across. The British wanted to gorge themselves on stuff that had been in short supply for years. You could not really blame them.

From 'little diamonds' successful companies grow!

The year 1866 was an important one in the history of Ogden of Harrogate. It was in this year that a son, James Roberts, was born to Charles and Ellen Ogden. Indeed, 27 years later in 1893, James founded his own business, The Little Diamond Shop and it is from this foundation that the business grew into the successful company it is today.

James' parents moved the family to Harrogate in 1867 in order to take advantage of the profitable area. It was whilst living at Oak Terrace that James developed his fascination with gem stones. The area was a source of quartz, which became known as 'Harrogate Diamonds' and were later sold by James in the early days of his business.

After leaving school James immediately set about learning the art of the jeweller and the watchmaker when he apprenticed himself to a Harrogate Jeweller, John Greenhalgh. John taught James everything he knew about precious stones and metals, and instructed him in the art of clock and watch construction. Sadly, in 1891 James' father died. However, this event gave James the opportunity he had been working for. He used some of his father's legacy to buy premises in Cambridge Street and on 27th April 1893 he opened his very first shop: The Little Diamond Shop.

At the time, Cambridge Street was one of the most important streets in the town and this, combined with James' brilliant customer relation skills, may have assisted in the initial success of the burgeoning business. Indeed, the first item to be sold was a hall clock to Smith Kelly for £2.12.6d. Other items sold in the first weeks included: earrings; pins; musical boxes; brooches; chains; and hair chains.

The emergence of Harrogate as a spa town brought many distinguished visitors to the town including many of the celebrated names of contemporary fashion. One fashionable craze,

Top left: The company founder, James R Ogden.
Above: An early advertisement. Below: The Cambridge Street shop circa 1900.

that of cycling, was introduced to Harrogate by these visitors. James was quick to pick up on this craze and made his shop the base for the exclusive Rudge British Safety Cycle Agency. Business began to flourish and only three years after the opening James was able to purchase the adjoining property in Cambridge Street and set about planning the layout of his expanded shop which opened in 1897 after a Great Clearance Sale.

By 1903, the business was doing so well that James could afford to take the risk of opening a new shop in Parliament Street which, with the addition of the new Kursaal, was increasing its importance as a prime retail area. In 1906 however, this shop was closed and another shop was opened, this time at 7 Cambridge Crescent. The same year also saw the opening of The Little Watch Shop at 33 Station Square to complement The Little Diamond Shop around the corner. Branches of the business were also opened at Bath, Llandrindod Wells, and Scarborough and as a result, 21 Cambridge Street was closed. This was a time of prosperity for the business and a Brighton publisher recognised this success stating that, 'Mr Ogden is a rare specialist, and no less so in the arts of working the precious metals'.

In 1910, Ogdens made one of its best ever investments. It purchased 38 James Street and closed the Station Square premises. This property was built by George Dawson to a design by Hirst of Bristol, and was of large and massive construction with four floors, a flat for a resident caretaker, and a rear workshop. A new shop interior was formed and the frontage was embellished by an elegant canopy to fit in with Harrogate's Edwardian fashions.

The advent of the first world war came as a terrible shock to the people of Harrogate who were used to having the crowned heads of Europe in their midst. Indeed, when James heard of the invasion of Belgium, whose King had visited the Royal Pump Room in the town, he was scandalised and converted his home into a reception centre for Belgian refugees. His work was rewarded after the war when he received the prestigious Legion d'Honneur. Unfortunately, the separate branches were closed at the outbreak of war and sadly, James' youngest son, Walter was killed at the battle of Cambrai at only 19 years of age.

Top: *Cars outside the Cambridge Street premises prior to a staff outing circa 1909.*
Top left: *J R Ogden and family after the formal awarding of the Honorary Freedom of the Borough.*
Right: *J R Ogden in the disguise he wore when looking for new premises in London.*

also saw Denis' son Glen, the great grandson of the founder, joining the business followed by his brother Jack. This ensured that the Company continued to prosper on the foundations established by earlier generations.

At the cessation of the war, James made the decision to incorporate the business as a Limited Company and open in London. To this aim, he disguised himself as a working class man and investigated potential sites in London to see if they were visited by wealthy people! Eventually, a shop was opened in Duke Street under the direction of his three sons, William, Jack and James R Ogden II. They made a success of the new shop, so much so, that in 1925 William left the Company to set up his own business.

During this period pearl jewellery started to rise in popularity and in its tradition of catering for the requirements of its customer, the Company even made a black pearl necklace commissioned by a recently widowed Lady for the sum of £16000! Amongst the many other interesting commissions was the most famous artefact to come from the Ogden workshops: the solid silver model of the Royal Pump Room which still graces the Mayor's table today.

In 1928 the Harrogate shop was enlarged by the purchase of the adjoining premises, No 40 James Street. Three years later a director, James' son Jack, was sent to London to manage the Duke Street shop, whilst the third brother, James II continued in the Harrogate business. In 1934, Jack's son, Guy, joined the Harrogate company, followed by his brother Denis and their cousin James R Ogden III, who joined his father in the Harrogate business.

In 1936, James Roberts Ogden was awarded the honorary Freedom of the Borough, recognising his contribution to local life. The year 1940 marked the end of an era. After disposing of his collection of books, antiquities and photographs to various libraries, James died. Sadly, his son Jack also died during this time when he was killed by an exploding bomb during the second world war.

Despite these setbacks, the business remained intact during the war under the leadership of James R Ogden II and later Denis, Guy and James R Ogden III (known as "Jim"). Indeed, at the cessation of the hostilities business began to thrive again and in the 1950s, at the behest of Sir Bernard Lomas, a splendid civic mace was made for presentation to Wellington in New Zealand. This decade

In 1980, Guy moved to Harrogate and Jack took over the management of the Duke Street premises until he left to concentrate on an academic career as the Director of the Cambridge Centre for Precious Metal Research. In 1982 Denis, Guy and Jim all retired and Denis' son Glen became Managing Director of the Company. The Company continued to go from strength to strength. In 1992, Ogdens of Harrogate Limited was able to celebrate its centenary year! Since then, many improvements and developments have taken place within the Company including the introduction of a special collection of jewellery in 1999 to commemorate the passing of the Millennium. Indeed, the Company continues to change with the times, adapting to the latest fashions and requirements of the customer without losing touch with the essential Ogden character, and whilst preserving the original Edwardian atmosphere of The Little Diamond Shop.

Top left: The shop at 40 James Street, occupied by Wilson & Son's pharmacy before being acquired by Ogdens in 1928. Top right:The second and third generations of the family: J R Ogden II (seated) with Denis, Guy and Jimmy. Below: Glen Ogden, who became Managing Director in 1982, with his wife Mary-Jane and their children.

Furnishing homes around Harrogate for four generations

The history of Smiths The Rink Limited is an interesting one which can be traced back all the way to the genteel days of Edwardian England, and more specifically to the Smith family of Harrogate.

Harrogate was an exciting place to live during the late 1800s and early 1900s. It was at this time, with the celebration of Queen Victoria's Diamond Jubilee and the British Empire at its pinnacle, that Harrogate too, was enjoying a time of prosperity. The new Royal Baths had been opened by his Royal Highness the Duke of Cambridge and their popularity led to Harrogate gaining the nickname of, 'The World's Greatest Spa'!

It was amongst this period of bustling progress and increasing prosperity that Frederick Smith decided he would play his part in reaping the rewards of the town's rapid development. He resolved to trust his entrepreneurial spirit and make his own contribution to Harrogate's success by setting up his own business. Consequently, in the year 1906 Frederick achieved his resolution and established his own second hand furniture business. Little did he realise then, that the business bearing his family name would still be flour-ishing four generations later under the name, Smiths The Rink Limited!

Perhaps it was inevitable that Frederick's business would be a great success. Indeed, before founding his second hand furniture firm, Frederick had accrued years of experience in the art of running a small business. He and his family lived in Skipton Street in Harrogate and it was from this street that Frederick successfully owned and ran a small fish and chip shop. The day that one of Frederick's customers asked him to do a big favour for them, proved to be a landmark day of paramount importance to the very existence of Smiths The Rink Limited. The favour in question was that Frederick displayed a side board in his shop window in order to advertise that it was for sale. Frederick complied and was amazed at how much the side board sold for. It was at this point that he decided he was in the wrong trade and began to devote his energies to setting up his own second hand furniture business. Eventually, Frederick located suitable premises in Harrogate at Bower Road. He sold his fish and chip shop, set up a second hand furniture shop from scratch, and opened for trade in 1906.

Bower Road proved to be an ideal site for Frederick's burgeoning business and he did indeed begin to reap

Below: Smiths premises in the early days.

These early years within the business, were invaluable to Thomas in his later, more senior role.

By 1928, Thomas had taken over the running of the business. It was in this year that Thomas began to implement a programme of expansion. Initially, he acquired number one Bower Road followed by numbers three and five which provided valuable extra space for the developing business. When number seven Bower Road came up for sale Thomas seized his opportunity. He purchased the house and converted it into another shop. The Smith family lived in the house above number one Bower Road and it was there that Thomas and his wife had a son, Reg.

the rewards of being located in the town of Harrogate. His second hand furniture business began to thrive and it was not long before Frederick became convinced that he had made the right decision in selling his fish and chip shop and changing trades. The first problem encountered by the business did not come until the advent of the first world war. Luckily for the business however, Frederick was by this time too old to be able to go to war. Although inevitably, business experienced a slight lull during this period, Frederick worked hard and managed to carry on trading throughout the war years.

After the cessation of the war Frederick's son, Thomas, was able to join his father in the family business. Thomas had in fact begun working for his father in 1917 but, when he reached the age of 18 a year later, he left the business in order to serve his country in the army during the war. It was not until his return, in 1918, that Thomas really began to play a full role within the business. At first, Thomas was occupied with helping his father wherever he could. Whether this included completing menial tasks, or the more interesting job of delivering or collecting goods with the help of the firm's horse and cart, Thomas proved to be eager and willing.

The 1930s were years of rapid growth for the business. The Smiths purchased their first petrol driven van at this time and hired their first employee. However, the most important event of the decade was the move, in 1935, to new premises at an old roller skating rink in Dragon Road from which the business continues to trade today under the name, Smiths The Rink Limited. The Smiths had previously rented the premises for storage purposes at a ridiculously low price, given because of the difficulty in converting the building for use.

Top and inset: Smiths "The Rink" premises prior to modernisation in the 1960s. Above left: The new shop facade circa 1962. Right:The opening ceremony of the extended premises in 1962.

However, before the premises could be put into full use as a showroom the second world war broke. The premises were requisitioned by the Ministry of Aircraft Production. Only a small strip was left from which to run the business. Thomas' daughters, Marjorie and Elsie, split their time between working in a munitions factory and helping their father. In this way, the business managed to survive during the war.

In 1946, the premises were returned for commercial use and the plans for expansion resumed. During the 1950s, the first Americans started to arrive in the town to buy antiques and it was during this decade that the company started to trade abroad, firstly in America, then Italy and the rest of Europe. In time to witness a new era of Freedom of Design, Thomas' son Reg, entered the business in 1950 at the age of 16 and started work, zooming to sales on his motorbike!

Business was booming and the new ranges stocked by the Company soon led to increasingly large customer demands. In order to cope with these demands, the Company doubled its showroom space to 30000 square feet by adding a second floor. This rebuilding was completed in 1962 and the improved premises were opened in a ceremony conducted by the Mayor. By the time the Company celebrated its Diamond anniversary at a dinner at Granby Hotel in 1966, business had continued to flourish, securing further success for the Smith family. Today, Smiths The Rink Limited employs

17 dedicated members of staff and has evolved into a blend of two separate aspects of the furniture business. Indeed, the business has now arrived at one of its most important stages of development. The running of the business has now been passed on to the fourth generation of Smiths. Reg's sons, Richard and Nicolas, now take care of the day to day running of Smiths The Rink Limited. Nicolas controls the internal management with emphasis on new furniture whilst Richard is responsible for the antique side of the business. This approach ensures that the unique blend of old and new for which The Rink has become renowned is maintained.

Top: *The new showrooms in the early 1960s.*
Below: *The shop in its most recent guise.*

A business tailored for success

It was perhaps inevitable that when the entrepreneurial William Grover Allen decided to set up his own business in the prosperous town of Harrogate, he would chose to establish it as a tailors and outfitters.

William's background was in this specific area of expertise. Ever since his birth in 1855, William had been surrounded by the tools of the trade due to the fact that his father, W F Allen, was the proprietor of a tailoring business based in Colchester, Essex. As soon as he had completed his education at the Colchester Grammar School, William eagerly embarked on the world of work in the town and eventually gained a job as a 'traveller' for a well known firm of outfitters. This job provided William with invaluable expertise and experience within the tailoring industry which he was to put to use in later years.

Indeed, it was whilst working as a 'traveller' that William first came to Harrogate. He was impressed by the town and immediately recognised that its passion for all things fashionable would provide ample potential for work within the tailoring trade. This it did, and on securing a job working for John Stokes, a tailor and outfitter based

Above: The company founder, W G Allen. Right: A military funeral arranged by W G Allen. Below: Staff outside the shop in the 1890s.

in High Harrogate (the fashionable part of town), William moved to Harrogate. It was not long before William's hard work and dedication made a good impression on John Stokes and when John opened a shop in the elite James Street, he appointed William as its manager!

Despite his promotion William's ambition would not allow him to rest on his laurels. He was eager to establish his own business and after marrying Emma Hiscoe and producing a son, William Hubert, this is exactly what William did. In 1880 William founded his own tailors and outfitters business at a lock-up shop in Parliament Street and so, Allen's was established. Initially business went well, however, when the Royal Baths were built William was forced to move his business across the street to number eight. This proved to be a minor hiccup and the move was temporary as it was soon possible to move to larger premises at number four Parliament Street.

Only eleven years after founding Allen's, the business became successful enough to justify expansion. In 1891, William purchased the five storey premises at 6 Prospect Crescent for the grand sum of £2530, gathered together with a little financial help from his mother! William set to work straight away and began using the

basement of the building as a workroom and stockroom and the ground floor as the shop and a cutting room. The other three floors of the building were sub-let to various businesses including the Harrogate Coal Company; the Crescent Athletic Club; and Mr Symington, a bookseller. The business received a considerable boost to its trade and soon became successful enough to be able to afford to purchase a motorcycle with a bassinet trailer. This in turn was replaced with a rather more sturdy Jowett two seater which was equipped with a hood and 'dickey seat'.

Allen's continued to thrive and as soon as it was possible William's son, William Herbert or Bert as he was known, joined his father in the business making it truly a family concern. Bert became involved in every aspect of the business, learning as much as he could about the trade. Indeed, it was not long before William could trust his son to take more and more responsibility within the business, leaving him more time to serve his community. William was an Honorary Superintendent

of the Harrogate Fire Brigade and the Harrogate Volunteer Salvage Corps; a town Councillor; Captain of the Harrogate Cycle Club; a founder of the Pannal and Oakdale Gold Clubs and St John's Ambulance Association; and a supporter of St Peter's Church. When, in 1931, he died William was also remembered as, 'one of the smartest men there were in the Borough'!

In his father's absence Bert was left to run Allen's and did so with the same ambition. He expanded the business to three floors devoted to a shoe department, a ready-to-wear department and a boys department and also brought the business through the second world war and its coupon system. When Bert died he left his sons, Jack and Bill, an extremely profitable business. Indeed, with over a century of hard work from the different Allen generations, and now in the hands of the fourth generation of the Allen family, Diana Wright and Elizabeth Stickney, Allen's of Harrogate has become one of the finest shops in the north of England, maintaining its reputation for quality and selling fine clothes, shoes, and luxury gifts.

Top: *The boys and youths department in the 1930s. Thousands of young customers have ridden the rocking horse.* **Above left:** *The men's clothing department.* **Right:** *Diana Wright and Elizabeth Stickney, the fourth generation of the Allen family.*

Drinka pinta milka day was an advertising slogan that appeared on billboards and television screens during the second half of the 20th century. The display in the Royal Hall was well aware of the value of dairy products in our diet. The style of container for milk had undergone dramatic changes over the years. The 1884 style of open jug and little churn was compared with the hygienic bottles of 1959. Milk is essentially an emulsion of fat and protein in water, along with dissolved sugar (carbohydrate), minerals and vitamins. What that means, in ordinary English, is that it is good for you. The health department was encouraging the public to drink milk, but was also advising playing safe. Untreated milk can

carry bacteria that will upset even the strongest of stomachs. It was about 100 years before this exhibition was mounted that Louis Pasteur introduced the treatment that was named after him. Pasteurisation was a method of raising the temperature of milk to a high temperature that would kill off the dangerous bugs. These days it has also been homogenised, a process that distributes the fat evenly. Although cows are the main source of the milk that we drink, other animals are important to other races. Sheep and goats are reared for their milk in southern Europe. The water buffalo is popular in Asia and the camel in Africa. Do you fancy a pint of semi skimmed dromedary milk? You would need a lot of bottle to drink it!

A driving force in Harrogate

Albert Hymas established his own business, now known as Albert Hymas Limited, in 1904. Albert's family came from Burton Leonard and for generations had owned J T Hymas, a well-boring company. However, the family firm went out of business some time after the last generation of Hymas' to inherit it, decided upon an alternative career as a vicar!

So, it was left to Albert to determine the profession of the next Hymas family business. As he was one half of a partnership working as a building firm, it was perhaps inevitable that when he decided to set out on his own, his business too would be part of the building trade. Initially, with the help of two labourers and a horse and cart, Albert did the stone work on a house a week in the Starbeck area. Albert ploughed all the money he earned back into the business. Indeed, with a payment of £50 per house Albert had, after three years of hard work, amassed enough income to be able to rent premises for the business. Thus, in 1907, Albert Hymas moved to a yard at Lynton Gardens. This move proved to be successful and by 1912, Albert was able to buy the business its first steam lorry. This purchase attracted a lot of attention in the local area and Albert received so many offers of work that they became a distraction from the building work. He even had to turn down the offer to set up a coach business as, being a religious man, he objected to working on Sundays.

In 1913 the business purchased its first petrol driven vehicle. This, in turn, led to the company's involvement with the Leeds Bradford Boiler Company as the vehicle was one of the few large enough to be able to transport the boilers! In this way the haulage side of the business began to develop. Despite this new direction, Albert remained a builder at heart and continued to

Above: Albert Hymas who founded his business in 1904. Below: One of the firm's trucks hauling a settling tank from Stanningley, near Leeds, to Northwich, Cheshire, for the Leeds & Bradford Boiler Company in April 1916.

undertake a hands-on role in the business. Indeed, he would often arrive in the office with his suit splattered in mud proudly announcing that, "The muck on this suit will pay for the next one"!

By 1915, Albert Hymas needed larger premises for its operations. These were found at The Grove, which was owned by a Lieutenant Sheepshanks. Interestingly, the deeds for The Grove were signed by the Lieutenant actually in the first world war trenches on the front-lines in France! After buying The Grove, Albert built two semi-detached houses on the site, lived in one and sold the other to the Methodists who still own it today. After the construction of a brick shed and an office was completed in 1916, the business moved into the new premises.

The year 1919 was an important one for the business. It was in this year that Albert's 19-year-old son, John Leslie (known as Leslie) joined the business after being de-mobbed from the army after only six months. Leslie started work as a bricklayer but eventually worked his way up into the office. Leslie built up the builders, merchant side of the business and by the 1920s the haulage side of the business was also thriving. It was also during these years that the stonework on the municipal buildings in Harrogate was completed by the firm.

The advent of the second world war brought with it another change to the composition of Albert Hymas. It

"Albert remained a builder at heart and continued to undertake a hands-on role in the business"

was at this time that the decision was taken to give up the building side of the business altogether. It was also during this time that Leslie took sole charge of the business from his father and developed the quarrying side of the business. As well as this extra responsibility, Leslie, who was by then too old for active service, volunteered as an Air Raid Warden and also allowed the business to carry out haulage work for the army.

In 1962, Leslie was joined in the business by his son, Michael, who became the third generation of Hymas to play a role in the company's history. After leaving school Michael had graduated from Durham University and then spent three years working for British Road Services. However, like his father, he started outside and gradually moved into the office.

After the war, the business continued to thrive and in the 1950s officially became a Limited Company. Today, the company comprises a mixture of four businesses including the haulage and the quarrying side of the business as well as a self drive business and property business which were added to the company during the 1980s. Indeed, with the help of its 20 employees, as it nears its 100th year, Albert Hymas Limited is hoping to continue to be a driving force in Harrogate.

Top: *An impressive line-up of the haulage fleet pictured in 1937.*

Valley Gardens, in a picture dating from the 1950s

Acknowledgments

North Yorkshire County Council Education & Library Services -
Harrogate Reference & Local Studies Department for the pictures on pages:
5 - 33, 46 - 71, 80 - 83, 92 & 93, 96
Margaret Power

Thanks are also due to
Andrew Mitchell who penned the editorial text and
Ann Ramsdale for her copywriting skills